ADVANCE PRAISE FOR

Why Is the Dalai Lama *Always Smiling?*

"Lama Tsomo builds a beautiful bridge between Western culture
and one of the most sophisticated ancient spiritual traditions
on Earth. Newcomers to Buddhist philosophy will find her
voice comforting and compassionate; expert practitioners
can still learn from her elegantly precise observations."

—MARTHA BECK, author of *Finding Your Own North Star*

"She writes as a Westerner who has found inner freedom through the
very same teachings and practices that help to keep such a beautiful
smile on His Holiness's faces … in spite of all of life's challenges.
Your understanding of our human predicament, and the path to lasting
happiness, will be richly enhanced by reading this lovely book."

—JOHN E. WELSHONS, author of
One Soul, One Love, One Heart and *Awakening From Grief*

"This book is excellent and would be helpful to a lot of
people who are keen to engage with Tibetan Buddhism
seriously as a practice and a way of being in the world."

—THUPTEN JINPA LANGRI, PH.D., Religious Studies;
English Translator for His Holiness the Dalai Lama

"This highly readable, extraordinarily informative and practical guide
by Lama Tsomo, an American female lama, is sprinkled with detailed
and specific instructions in Tibetan Buddhist meditation practices and
with concrete suggestions for promoting happiness and well–being."

—RICHARD J. DAVIDSON, founder, Center for Investigating Healthy
Minds, University of Wisconsin–Madison

"In today's fast-paced, high-tech world, the struggle to find truth
and meaning requires a special kind of teacher. Thank goodness
for the arrival of Lama Tsomo, whose insights
and instruction could not have come at a better time."

—VAN JONES, host, *Crossfire* (CNN)

"Before Lama Tsomo, I felt meditation was only in the mind. Through these practices, I felt it come into my heart. Through Lama Tsomo, I found more freedom, laughter and grace. I honor her as a teacher and am grateful she has brought these ideas into a format that is accessible to more people."

—MARIANNE MANILOV, student of Lama Tsomo; founder, Engage Network

"Lama Tsomo's conversational style and clarity, open-mindedness yet dedication all contribute to a book that will meet the needs of a great many who seek to deepen their inner life but are unsure how."

—ARTHUR ZAJONC, PH.D., President, Mind & Life Institute

"An accessible and engaging exploration of the tried and true fundamentals of meditation as they've been handed down through the millennia."

—ARIANNA HUFFINGTON, founder, *The Huffington Post*

"Designed for readers from all backgrounds and levels of experience, this beautiful book offers step-by-step guidance in accessible practices, as well as a rich array of stories, scientific perspectives and ways of dealing with challenges that arise on the path. You will find in these pages a precious invitation to inhabit the happiness, love and freedom of your own awakened heart."

—TARA BRACH, PH.D., author of *Radical Acceptance* and *True Refuge*

"Especially timely now, when there is so much need for spiritual remedy in this age of increasing inner emptiness in the midst of excessive materialism imbued with collective neurosis."

—ANAM THUBTEN, author of *No Self, No Problem*

Especially geared for North American wisdom seekers and written in friendly and understandable language, the book serves up a rich feast of abundant and clearly explained practices. Given the perilousness of our times, Lama Tsomo offers an exciting and needed gift of deeper soul journeying into an inner peace and joy.

—THE REV. DR. MATTHEW FOX, author of *Occupy Spirituality* and *Meister Eckhart*

Why Is the
Dalai Lama
Always Smiling?

A Westerner's Introduction and Guide
to Tibetan Buddhist Practice

By Lama Tsomo

Namchak

PUBLISHING

Namchak

PUBLISHING

The Namchak Foundation supports the study and practice of
the Namchak Lineage to Tibetan Buddhism. Namchak.org.

Library of Congress Control Number: 2014945034

Book design and typography by Mary Ann Casler
Cover art by Adam Agee for Creative Studios International LLC
Cover Photo © 2007 Alison Wright
Editorial by Michael Frisbie

Cataloging-in-Publication Data
is available from the Library of Congress

First printing, March 2016
ISBN: 978-0-9905711-0-0
Printed in Hong Kong on recycled paper

10 9 8 7 6 5 4 3 2 1

Contents

Tonglen 193

Doing Daily Practice 207

In Closing: Some Words of Advice 219

Interestingly, there was no blue light in the room when I took this picture. I know because it was my own kitchen. It only appeared when we developed the film. —LAMA TSOMO

Homage

In the Tibetan tradition, I want to begin by paying homage to my Root Lama, Gochen Tulku Sangak* Rinpoche, who has guided me with patience, wisdom, and a good helping of humor, since the beginning of my pursuit of the Vajrayana path. Studying at his feet has been like standing with my mouth open, under a waterfall. As with glaciers flowing to waterfalls, truth and inspiration flow in abundance from the Buddha, through the masters of this lineage, and through Rinpoche. I continue to receive this gift in wonder and gratitude.

---

* Sometimes spelled Sang-Ngag.

"When the iron eagle flies and horses run on wheels,
the Tibetan people will be scattered over the earth,
and the Dharma will go to the land of the red man."

—*Prediction by Padmasambhava, the enlightened Indian master
who caused Buddhism to take root in Tibet in the ninth century, A.C.E.*

KHEN RINPOCHE

Acknowledgments

It seems only right to begin with my family. My parents permanently infected me with the joy of exploring the nature of reality and understanding people. During my growing-up years, my sister sat with me for hours as we passionately replicated that pursuit. She's the real writer in the family, not to mention a brilliant editor, but she's always graciously encouraged my efforts.

I also want to thank Herman Schaalman, my family's rabbi, who gave me my first guidance and pointed me in the right direction in my pursuit of wisdom.

Two more whom I wish to acknowledge are my dogs. They have been my constant, loving companions throughout the entire, years-long journey of writing this book … well, except for one writing stint at the monastery in Nepal. I deeply regretted that they were too big to fit in my carry-on bag.

I feel a great deal of gratitude for my editor, Michael Frisbie, who is not only top-notch at the art of editing, but a natural and accomplished educator. Given that this was my first real attempt at a full-length book, I needed both of those gifts in great measure. Had it not been for him, this book would have been just a nice manual. That is what I'd originally had in mind. But because of his genuine enthusiasm for the material (despite not being a Buddhist) and his skills, his questions and comments evoked the rest of this book, which was actually in there somewhere. He always gave generously, and with good humor. Actually a hysterical sense of humor!

Huge thanks to Mary Ann Casler for her lovely work on the design, layout, and images for the book. She guided us expertly through the galley and print process, as well as myriad details involved in publishing a book. Thanks to Jason Hicks, aided and abetted by Deborah Hicks, in the recording of this entire book—no small feat! Gratitude to JoAnn Hogan for managing the countless details necessary for the success of this project.

Arthur Zajonc, emeritus professor of physics at Amherst, was kind enough to read and comment on the physics tidbits. Dr. Richard Davidson, one of the scientists in the Mind & Life Institute working with His Holiness the Dalai Lama XIV, and head of the Center for Investigating Healthy Minds and of the Waisman Center at the University of Wisconsin–Madison, took precious time from his busy schedule to talk to me and review my neuroscience pieces.

Lama Chönam and Sangye Khandro, co-founders of the Light of Berotsana translation group, read an early version of my manuscript and gave me lots of crucial feedback, corrections, and encouragement. Tulku Anam Thubten Rinpoche, from whom I've been fortunate enough to receive teachings, read and gave me helpful comments and great encouragement on my nearly finished manuscript. Also in the Experts on Tibetan Buddhism camp was Namchak Dorlop (full name Namchak Dorje Lopön Choeji Lodoe),

Tulku Sangak Rinpoche's brother, who reviewed the manuscript for accuracy.

I feel these acknowledgments must include—and highlight—the masters of the Namchak Lineage, our particular branch of the larger Nyingma Lineage, beginning with Nup Sangye Yeshe, who hid the teachings, then Tsasum Lingpa, who later revealed those teachings, continuing in an unbroken thread of wisdom, down to the present world lineage holder, Tulku Sangak Rinpoche, to whom this book is dedicated. The most recent revealer of the teachings of our lineage was Pedgyal Lingpa, who passed them directly to Tulku Sangak Rinpoche. Without them, I would not have received the gems that I talk about in this book. A lineage of teachings that is revealed and passed down in this way is referred to as a *treasure*. And that's actually an understatement.

I wouldn't want to receive all that Rinpoche and those who came before have offered me and not transmit what I can. Whenever I felt my lack of readiness too keenly, I also had this thought: if I had come upon this book when I was much younger, I know that I would have been delighted to use it as a beginning. If this book turns out to be of benefit to you, then my purpose for writing it will have been fulfilled.

THE DALAI LAMA

FOREWORD

As our world becomes ever more connected, the world's great spiritual traditions are able to get to know each other better. This provides their followers opportunities to learn from one another and develop a deeper appreciation and respect for each other's teachings, traditions and practices. I, for one, have learned a great deal from the insights of spiritual traditions other than my own.

I often describe myself as a staunch Buddhist. However, I have never felt the urge to propagate Buddhism with the aim of converting others to my point of view. In general, I believe it's better and safer for most people to stay within the religious tradition of their birth. The world's faiths evolved in specific geographical and cultural circumstances, which gives them an affinity to the spiritual inclinations and needs of specific communities. I am quite open about this, especially when I am asked to speak about Buddhism in the West, where the main spiritual traditions are historically Judeo-Christian.

At the same time, I recognize that, especially in today's interconnected world, there will be individuals who find the approache of traditions other than those to which they were born to be more effective and suited to their own spiritual aspirations. I know many people in the West, in both North America and Europe, who engage in serious study and practice of Buddhist teachings. They find the advice for training the mind presented in the Buddhist teachings to be profoundly beneficial and meaningful. Some such Western Buddhists have been steadfast in their commitment to their Buddhist practice for several decades, demonstrating a deep dedication. It is in this context that I am happy to see the publication of this new book *A Westerner's Introduction and Guide to Tibetan Buddhism*. Written by Sangak Tsomo, a long-time student and practitioner of Tibetan Buddhism, the book outlines the basic views of the Tibetan tradition and examples of some of its practices for the interested modern reader. I am pleased to note that while the author describes her personal journey into Buddhism in some detail, she continues to honor her traditional Jewish heritage.

I have no doubt that Western readers who wish to deepen their understanding of Tibetan Buddhist practices will find much to interest them here, and that members of other faiths, or even those who have none, will enjoy this sincere account of spiritual exploration.

June 6, 2014

Pema Khandro Ling
1221 Luisa Street, Suite A
Santa Fe, NM 87505
santafe@ewam.org

Nyingma School of Tibetan Buddhism

Ewam Sang-ngag Ling
PO Box 330 Arlee, MT 59821
406.726.0217 • www.ewam.org
admin@ewam.org

Gochen Tulku Sang-ngag Rinpoche
Spiritual Director

Foreword

For the benefit of Westerners who are beginners in the practice of Buddhism, Lama Tsomo has drawn on her own knowledge of Western and Eastern ways of thinking and devoted all her efforts to writing this current work, in order to provide a bridge that will forge a connection between these cultures. I am delighted that she has completed this book, and offer my sincere and heartfelt thanks and best wishes to her in this endeavor.

On this note, let me say a few words about Lama Tsomo, the author of this book, since she is a personal student of mine. Beginning with our initial meeting in 1995, she undertook the study and practice of the Buddhist teachings, including her spending two or three months each year in strict retreat, in addition to maintaining an uninterrupted daily practice. In this way, she has dedicated herself enthusiastically to completing a system of training from the preliminary stages up to and including the advanced yogic disciplines (*tsa-lung*) and Dzogchen practices.

On the basis of her efforts, in 2005 I formally recognized Lama Tsomo's accomplishments in an investiture ceremony that took place in conjunction with the graduation of the nuns who participated in the three-year retreat program at my meditation center of Kusum Khandro Ling in Pharping, Nepal.

Following this, in 2006, on the occasion of the final year of the intensive study program at Ewam Sang-ngag Ling in Arlee, Montana, I conferred on Lama Tsomo the formal title of a lama of the Ewam Foundation.

She has now authored this book to introduce people to the Buddhist teachings, in order to help new practitioners on into the future. I encourage all to read and study this text with a sense of trust in its usefulness, and am sure that they will profit greatly through such efforts. Please take this advice to heart.

This was written in my retreat cabin by the teaching throne of Longchenpa at Ewam Pema Khandro Ling, by me, the sixth holder of the title of Gochen Tulku.

Sang-ngag Tenzin
April 2014

~ Ewam Nepal ~
Turquoise Leaf Nunnery - Phone: 977-1-710-094/Sang-ngag Phurba Ling Retreat Center - Phone: 977-1-710-093
POB 7032 Devi G.B.S. Pharping Kathmandu, Nepal

Ewam is a federally registered 501(c)(3) US non-profit organization

WHO IS LAMA TSOMO?

And Why Should I Listen to Her?

As you read this book, you will come to
know Lama Tsomo well: not just her
teachings, but her "story"—the personal
and spiritual path that led her to
this book, and to you.

Before you begin, though, you may be curious about her credentials. So here is a brief overview, highly condensed, that by no means contains the full breadth of her training and accomplishments but should give you a good idea of her qualifications as your guide.

A more detailed curriculum vitae is included at the end of the book.

—Editor

Lama Tsomo's Background

- A total of three years of strict, solitary retreat under the guidance of Tulku Sangak Rinpoche, progressing through all stages of the Vajrayana path.
- Thirty 1- to 2-week training/study intensives with Tulku Sangak Rinpoche and Khen Rinpoche (full name Namchak Khenpo Rinpoche Ngawang Gelek).
- 2005, lama ordination, by Rinpoche.
- Rinpoche has requested that Lama Tsomo teach the practices in this book, as well as the Preliminary Practices, or Ngöndro.
- Received all of the transmissions (both *wang* and *lung*) of the Namchak Lineage from Rinpoche.
- Fifteen years teaching Vajrayana (Tibetan) Buddhism and related courses in Taiwan, Hong Kong, Montana, California (including Stanford University), and at the Houston Jung Center, Wisdom University, the Academy for the Love of Learning in New Mexico, and University of Missoula Graduate School of Social Work.
- DVD series of dialogues with Christian theologian Matthew Fox.
- Speaks fluent Tibetan, and has translated for Tulku Sangak Rinpoche and Khen Rinpoche.
- M.A. in Counseling Psychology from Antioch University.
- Five years of private practice as a psychotherapist seeing clients.
- Author of numerous articles on Tibetan Buddhism.

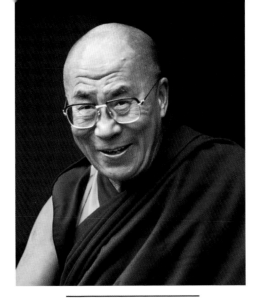

PROLOGUE

Why IS the Dalai Lama Always Smiling?

In looking at His Holiness' life, we wouldn't automatically assume he's had reason to be happy all the time. He's had his share of serious health problems, for one thing. He's lost his country, his people have suffered terribly, he has lived in exile, helpless as his people's culture and wisdom tradition are being lost. And his crushing schedule would burn out people half—a *third*—his age.

Yet, smile he does. Constantly. Hour after hour, year after year, no matter what happens. Although he is unquestionably a heavy-weight scholar and master practitioner, his constant joyfulness is palpable. His infectious laugh rolls out at the slightest provocation, and he jokes quite a bit, himself … then laughs at his own jokes!

This is not because he forgets the plight of his people, or sweeps his own suffering under the rug. When a nun, Ani Tenzin Palmo, spoke to him about the plight of women who had been trying to devote their lives to the *Dharma* with almost no support from the lamas, His Holiness burst into tears on the spot. He resolved that far greater opportunities had to be provided for women to reach the heights of scholarship and practice that men had been supported in pursuing.

Meanwhile, the sun came out shortly after that, and he was smiling again … while not forgetting his resolution. He has indeed—of course—followed through, and much progress has been made since then.

If you were to ask His Holiness why he smiles, of course I can't predict what he'd say. But judging from his writings and from witnessing him personally many times, I would say this:

He has plumbed the depths of understanding the nature of the universe and the nature of the mind. He has trained his own mind—both brain and heart. He has concluded that we are not separate from each other, as we so persistently think we are. I believe he lives within a view that holds the truth of our common root of being. He sees this as an ongoing reality, and stands in that reality.

Compassion, then, comes quite naturally if a person lives from

that reality. And so does joy. He doesn't have to busy himself with "looking out for number one." (Or, to put it another way, the "one" he is looking out for is the "one" that is, ultimately, all of us.) Imagine that. What a *relief*! What *freedom*.

Every day he spends several hours in our universal "home"— that great ocean of compassionate awareness that I've spoken of. After his morning meditation, everywhere he looks he sees with a clean lens, so he perceives something close to the exquisitely beautiful *pureland* and pure inhabitants that are the true nature of things. Everything around him is alive. He sees each of us as another beautiful wave in the constant "dis*play*" of that great ocean. He sees the relatively tiny significance of his own wave-existence.

And remember, within and throughout that whole ocean … is *joy*. The kind we never have to depart from, even at death.

The Buddha has invited us home and shown us the way. Won't you come along?

INTRODUCTION

✸ *Why This Book*

This book grew out of a course that I taught, wryly titled *Tibetan Buddhism—Why Bother?* I figured we Westerners don't automatically know why we should, so I might as well come right out with it. As I taught the course, I assigned the occasional book, always on the lookout for more. The students benefited from those books, but there was still a particular book I was looking for, but never found. So I finally decided to write it myself!

I'd originally intended to write a book only as a study guide and reference for the course, but as I kept thinking of more and more things to introduce, and helpful hints from my experience, it naturally evolved into something larger. After all, I can only teach so many people in a course in Montana. I decided to grow it into a package that could serve as a fuller introduction for people who couldn't come to my classes. The outcome is this kit, as well as another book to follow, and then one after that.

I had been looking for a book that introduced Westerners to the Vajrayana (Tibetan) Buddhist view of reality, the context for the practices, and the actual practices themselves, along with advice from Westerner to Westerner on how to use the methods effectively. There were parts of most of this in one book or another, but a student would really have to dig through these various books. And sometimes the practices or the advice was explained in Tibetan vocabulary or based on assumptions that would be shared by a Tibetan audience but unfamiliar to Westerners. Even if the books were meant for a Western audience, if the author was a Tibetan, most of my students, who were completely new to the subject, had trouble relating to the material.

For example, almost any Tibetan master will begin a teaching by saying something like, "And keeping in mind, all motherly sentient beings...." This makes perfect sense to Tibetans. Are you a bit confused? In my course I explained that in Tibetan cosmology, we've all been incarnating forever, since the incalculable beginning of time. That being the case, we've all most likely incarnated in all possible permutations at least once. It would logically follow that, at some point, every single creature had been our mother. Therefore we want to listen and apply these teachings so that we can become buddhas ourselves, and really be of help to all our former mothers. There's even more to that phrase than I've just elucidated, but you get the idea. Tibetans almost universally feel great love, respect, and compassion for their mothers. Of the many strong emotions Westerners feel toward their mothers, those may not be the primary ones. If with just that first sentence the newcomers are lost, you can imagine how the rest of the talk tends to go.

After a short time with students I was able to give them a "ramp up" so that they could connect more fully with my Root Lama,* Tulku Sangak Rinpoche,** and other Tibetan masters, and receive the profound benefits they had to offer.

---

* A spiritual guide and mentor. The relationship of Root Lama to student is a deeply intimate one, for the lama introduces the student not only to the teachings and practices, but, over the years, to the very nature of mind and reality.

** Rinpoche is a title given to especially accomplished lamas.

For some reason, I usually found Rinpoche easy to relate to, and had the unbelievable good fortune and luxury of extensive time with him for questions and discussions. But most students couldn't learn from him until I'd built some bridges for them. For one thing, Rinpoche doesn't speak English, and I've learned Tibetan.

Most people don't have the time, interest, or proclivity for learning Tibetan. Oh, if ONLY there were a Tibetan language pill!

For many of the core ideas in Tibetan Buddhism, we Westerners just don't have the "receptors" to cognize the concepts, envision the world-view, understand relationships, and work with fundamental archetypes. My studies in psychology, particularly Jungian psychology, have been some help. And all the time I've spent doing the practices—often intensely immersed in them—has been extremely helpful too.

I've been very satisfied, doing the work of being a bridge to Rinpoche and the vast treasure of wisdom he carries, connecting with students in the way that I can, because of what I carry. As a matter of fact, I see this as my life's primary purpose for my remaining years.

❊ *Using This Book*

If, as you read this book, the ideas make sense to you, I really recommend that you not leave it in the intellectual realm. Actually try the first practice for a while. Once you feel comfortable with that and have gained some benefit, you might feel ready to add the next one. Tibetan Buddhism isn't just a way of thinking, or feeling; it's a way of being and acting.

The Tibetan texts always remind us of the three essential facets of the path to enlightenment: *study, contemplate, meditate*. I suggest the same progression, in bite-size pieces. Read a bit; reflect; then try the practice.

Even as you're just reading, pause and reflect: take a break, a breather, a breath. This book is designed to be absorbed thoughtfully and deliberately. There's no prize for sprinting to the last page, but there are many rewards for proceeding slowly and lingering thoughtfully, reflecting not only on what I've brought to the page but on what *you* bring to the experience of this book.

Though the pages are numbered (and as you'll see, Buddhists *love* numbering things), the book itself is not strictly linear. It offers principles and observations, not a recipe. You may find that your first glimpse of an idea piques your interest, which is then further illuminated by a fuller explanation or a different perspective, a chapter or two down the path—kind of like life, don't you think?

That said, when it comes to learning the practices, you'll want to gain some ability with the foundational ones before moving on to more advanced ones. You'll get far more enlightenment mileage out of exploring this text and related media, reading the recommended books, and doing the practices for about a year, than—for example—immediately forging ahead from one set of practices to the next.

Let's say you wanted to become good at math and had just read through a textbook on addition and subtraction. What if you then just pushed straight on and started reading about the next levels, right up to spherical trigonometry? You wouldn't even have gotten good at addition and subtraction because you didn't take the time to practice until you were solid in those fundamentals. Then and only then could you do multiplication, then division. Without gaining solid ability in simple algebra, there's no hope of your ever getting good at spherical trigonometry. Training your mind works pretty much the same way.

As you read and reflect, you may well ask yourself, "Why should I believe all this stuff just because she's telling me it's true?" And the answer is, you shouldn't.

Early in my studies with Rinpoche, he clarified a foundational point to me. He told me that *what he was teaching me was not a religion, but a set of highly effective, proven methods for improving my mind.* Eventually, if I followed them and succeeded, they would lead me to full enlightenment.

This assurance was important to me, because I didn't want to have to give up being Jewish, and at that point I didn't know whether I automatically, instantly—or ever, maybe—was going to buy into everything in Tibetan Buddhism. At that point I was only at the stage of having

What he was teaching me was not a religion, but a set of highly effective, proven methods for improving my mind.

road tested some of the methods and having liked the results. I was relieved to hear where Rinpoche was coming from on this point. I was a psychotherapist on my quest to find the world's best proven and provable methods for making myself and others better, happier people. If I could reach enlightenment, so much the better.

Now I'm saying the same thing to you: that you don't have to take anything on blind faith. The Buddha made it very clear that blind faith is an inferior kind and that the conviction born of inquiry made with our eyes open, the conviction born of our own experience, is the very best, most unshakable faith.

I've written *Why Is the Dalai Lama Always Smiling?* in a series of semi-retreats, where I do practice sessions in the early mornings and after dinner. For the later morning and afternoon sessions I've usually been writing this book sitting on a mountain, with my dogs sleeping nearby. I spent one of these retreats at Rinpoche's convent in Nepal. I've thoroughly enjoyed the process, and I've found that much of the book has poured out of me with relative ease. Little wonder, since I've articulated these ideas and been working with new students for all this time.

I find the balance of practice and writing to be complementary. The practice helps the writing, and the offering of this book, being an act of generosity, which is a buddha quality, strengthens my practice. The benefits go in all directions, including yours, I hope.

As I write this, I imagine I'm talking to you at my mountain retreat.

My aspiration is that you benefit somehow from this book, even if you don't agree with all the concepts, or decide, for now, to tread only part of this whole path. Perhaps some piece of it rings true for you, or you do one practice for some time and it helps. That's enough to make it worthwhile for me to write it and you to read it. So, again, take the book in small sips, turning the concepts over in your mind, trying out the practices for yourself.

And in the process … *enjoy.*

✦ *Are You as Happy as You Want to Be?*

If you're always completely happy, this book is probably not for you.

We all want to be happy and don't want to suffer. That's true not only for us humans, but for dogs, cats, mice, and their fleas. Yet try as we might, we can't seem to work it out to always be completely happy. In the West it was long thought that you were born either a happy person or not. Even scientists held the firm conviction that the brain changed very little after early childhood. Many recent scientific studies, particularly in brain plasticity, have turned that conviction, well, on its head.

Many of these studies compared longtime Buddhist practitioners of various nationalities with novices or non-practitioners and found positive changes of all sorts in the brain. The longtime practitioners' readings were such as had never before been recorded in a laboratory. Scientists also found that the longer the subjects had practiced, the more extraordinary the readings. Among the positive changes recorded in the experiments were improved ability to focus on a task, increased size in desirable parts of the brain, off-the-charts readings in gamma waves (which are good thing), evidence of ongoing improved mood, and improved longevity factors. The clear trend was that the longer a person had been practicing these techniques, the more marked these positive changes were.

The Buddha had set out to provide humanity with methods to achieve ultimate, lasting happiness. Had he really found the secret to happiness, after all? Could his methods work for everyone?

Although those practitioners with off-the-charts readings had practiced many, many hours, studies also discovered that ordinary Westerners who tried these techniques began to show improvement right away.* When I came upon these methods, I found that they truly worked for me. After sampling all of the major branches

---

* One example, among several, is the Shamata Project, a joint project with the Santa Barbara Institute for Consciousness, University of California–Davis, and Shambhala Mountain Center. The project is centered primarily at UC Davis.

of Buddhism, I felt the most affinity for Tibetan Buddhism, called *Vajrayana*. I'll explain a bit more about the distinctions between those major branches a bit later. This book is an introduction specifically to Tibetan Buddhism, or the Vajrayana Buddhist view and practice. The practices meet us as we are right now, and lead us toward nothing less than ultimate, permanent happiness.

If we really stop and think about it, everything we do all day long is devoted either to pursuing happiness or eliminating suffering. Even when we work grueling hours at a job we hate? Well, why wouldn't a person quit? Because they would rather eat and feed their family. If there were a happier work situation for them, then they probably would quit in favor of that.

One fellow I know joined the army, not because he expected a picnic, but because it was worth the hardship for him to feel the satisfaction of serving his country. We often go through hardship to make others happy, because the satisfaction makes us happy. It's worth it.

If we don't have a choice that offers 100% happiness, we settle for the best we can get. We pick one choice because we think it will make us relatively happier than any alternatives we see.

We may have times in our lives when we manage to have a lot of what we want. Even then, some of us will fixate on what we *don't* have, on the glass being 5% empty instead of 95% full.

And even if we succeed in being happy for a short time, the happiness evaporates all too soon and we find ourselves suffering. Even if we hold suffering at bay for a time, it eventually catches up with us. One classic example is romantic love. Although the movies may show the couple riding off into the sunset at the end, after a few years of marriage or living with someone, it can feel a little—or a lot—less heavenly. I often tried to imagine what would have happened if Romeo and Juliet had lived and gotten married. Then they have kids, argue over how to discipline them, fight about money, and really part ways when he has an affair.

I knew a couple who enjoyed many years of relative marital happiness. Then the husband died. This one is inescapable. We all die. The comedian Louis C.K. notes that if you're lucky "you'll meet the perfect person, who you love infinitely, and you even argue well, and you grow together, and you have children, and then you get old together, and then she's going to die … that's the best case scenario: you're going to lose your best friend."

We're usually shocked and often indignant ("Why me?!") when happy times come to an end … forgetting, again and again, that everything comes to an end. Yet we know this from both science (entropy) and personal observation.

How can a set of methods help us to be happy, even when life is full of difficulties and pain? We all constantly try to change the outer circumstances, but they're often beyond our control. Often our inner ones are too. We can't let go of a grudge, though carrying it does us no good. We can't stop yearning for someone we

love, who doesn't share our feelings. We can't stop wishing that the world were different, and that we were different in the world.

This book brings you the Vajrayana perspectives on all this and introduces you to a set of methods that have helped millions of people over thousands of years. In this book I explain only the foundational methods, but with just these simple practices, many have reported huge benefits. These methods have changed lives. Not only have these changes been substantiated in various controlled studies, but I've heard the same news again and again from my students, after doing these very exercises for just a few months.

There are many real examples of practitioners who have followed this entire path, with all kinds of astonishing results. Some practitioners have even transformed their bodies out of the material realm altogether, with rainbow-colored light streaming out of their empty clothes as they attained complete enlightenment. A rather dramatic proof of Einstein's theory equating matter with light, wouldn't you say? On a more modest yet inspiring note, my teacher, Tulku Sangak Rinpoche, managed to transform his experience of being imprisoned as a spiritual leader from abject misery to true happiness.

Since Rinpoche took me on as his first American "guinea pig," he spent a great deal of time teaching me these methods so that I too could be happy in nearly any circumstance. (I think he was also sometimes thinking, "Let's see how this American does with THIS practice!") I tried the methods for myself and found that they really worked. Though I'm nowhere near perfecting the practices, I'm already much happier, and live with much more skill and aplomb—especially in life's most challenging times—than I did before. I've continued to make steady progress over the years, and I want nothing more than to pass these gems of wisdom and techniques on to anyone interested … *you*.

WHY I BOTHERED

Maybe it will help you to relate to all this as a Westerner if I share a little about my own spiritual and personal journey and how I found my way here.

The Early Years: Even Then, I Was on a Path

I might as well start at the beginning. I was born. This happened in 1953, just after my parents had moved to a small town in the Midwest. We were on the edge of town, on a gravel road, across from a golf course. I loved wandering around outside, playing with my dog, and thrashing with abandon in mud puddles (much to my mother's horror). I still remember the wonder of my mother's garden producing delicious food, and my father planting a tree that *apples* would come from. I was grief-stricken when we moved to the inner city of Chicago, before I turned five. The sound of the breeze in tree branches was replaced by traffic noise. I could hardly see the sky.

When I was seven, I told my mother that when I grew up I would live in the country, with lots of animals and a big garden.

She said, in effect, "There, there, dear. You'll probably marry a (nice, Jewish) businessman and live in the city, where he can have an office." That would have been a living death for me. A woman who worked for my family and was like another parent, raising me, had grown up on a family homestead, and I loved hearing her stories about that life. I have indeed lived in the country for most of my adult life, with animals and a big garden.

It wasn't an intellectual decision for me to live in the country, in the midst of nature. I just loved such places. Actually, it was only in the few years I lived in a city that I had to make a decision that went against my natural grain. Why would anyone want to live in a city? And why wouldn't I want to live where there is stunning beauty in all directions?

I don't know why trees are shaped so beautifully, and move so gracefully in the wind, or why I see them as beautiful. Why are owls dressed in such exquisitely fine and subtle designs, marked just so, around their eyes? Why do I marvel when I see them? I don't really have an answer for all these questions, but my best working hypothesis is that, through countless generations, I was genetically designed to love these things, and to love living from my garden. Humans evolved high on the food chain, so we've been in the minority among the world's population ever since our beginning. I feel most comfortable living where humans are in the minority.

When I was about to move to a more rural place than ever, where those beautiful owls make their home, a woman asked me, "I thought you already did the 'back to the earth' thing. Why are you doing this now?" I was too polite to reply, "I'm *from* earth. And you?"

Though the Tibetan texts urge us to live in a quiet place, free of human society, my choosing rural life wasn't done with gritted teeth, because I thought it was good for me or virtuous. It was, well, natural.

Being born Jewish, I certainly could have turned to my own rich tradition for spiritual training. My rabbi was a truly wise, learned, and kindhearted man. My experience at Sunday school, though, was absolutely meaning-free. The well-intentioned teachers there taught us Hebrew (which, if you're exposed to once a week, you're guaranteed never to learn), Jewish history, and Jewish songs. I was truly hoping for some pearls of wisdom about how life works, and how I could work with life. I was bored and frustrated. My brother and I would hide when the carpool came to pick us up. During the fifteen-minute recess I'd race to the library and read Bible stories. I checked out books and soaked in the nourishing wisdom embedded in the stories. After those precious fifteen minutes, I dragged my feet back to class.

After a year or two of my begging not to go to temple, my parents stopped making me. Regular school was also nearly meaning-free. So was TV, and nearly everything around me. I found some solace in music and reading, but mostly felt bereft. It wasn't until college that I discovered avenues for pursuing real meaning.

The entire time I was growing up, I was exposed to another Western tradition for exploring the world: science. My father had a passion for it. Often his "bedtime story" for me was a lesson on Einstein's Theory of Relativity, or the construction of atoms, or modern genetics. He was so impassioned about science, and so good at rendering it in a way I could understand, that I was caught up in the adventure of inquiry. He would pull out textbooks and point while I looked on, making it all come to life. I was so infected by his delight and awe at the workings of the universe, that I think he shared this particular subject more with me than with my siblings. Though I didn't become a scientist, in my keen interest in the subject, I carry that legacy to this day.

On the occasional Saturday, my father and I might go to the local planetarium, where they taught about astronomy as we sat in the dark—planets, stars, and constellations perfectly represented above. They could fast-forward a thousand years into the future, or turn back to the sky at the time of Christ. They projected photographs of supernovas, and explained how we could determine the chemical makeup of distant stars. I was riveted. Dad was too … until his tiredness succumbed to the dark room and the soothing voice. He invariably nodded off, snoring loudly enough for me to have to elbow him.

In junior high and high school, I was kind of a wallflower. There were several cliques, of course, as with any modern American school. I wasn't exactly *out* of the cliques but I wasn't exactly *in* a particular one, either—I had friends here and there, in various cliques, which I preferred. Almost every day I would stand in the lunchroom with my tray, looking at each of the tables with each of the cliques, wondering who I would sit with that day. Would it be Carla, who was sitting with the uncool, artist clique? Or Jane, who was with her clique—the class brains/geeks? Or Becca, who was in the almost-in group? I slid through it all, hardly noticed. That would include boys. I had almost no dates. I wasn't the type to want to go to parties and be "in." I had enough friends to be content with my social life, other than wishing for a boyfriend, of course.

My childhood had been a depressing experience for me. I had grown up in a family that had all its physical requirements taken care of, but not all our emotional needs. I felt close to my father, but he had to travel constantly for his work and, even when in town, worked long hours at the office.

Children, especially young children, need their parents to be perfect and godlike, and even as we grow up, we may expect parental perfection. My parents were good-hearted but neurotic human beings, trying their best, just like all the rest of us. They each blessed me with wonderful gifts, but they also committed sins of omission and commission. I grew up a neurotic mere human as well, and raised my own children imperfectly—guaranteed.

As children, we all suffer from that huge divide between what we want/need, and what our very human parents can give. As I was growing up, I suffered from that too, in many ways.

Throughout my childhood I felt lonely, sad, and not very safe. I used to cry for no apparent reason, and I was just waiting to graduate high school and leave home. The underlying tone of that time was a melancholic longing, though I didn't even know for *what*.

These circumstances—the suffering in and around me, these gaps, my sense of not being connected—motivated me to search, though at first I wasn't really sure what I was searching *for* to ease my loneliness and longing.

I remember riding on the bus one day in junior high, thinking, "If I could just not feel the bad feelings and only feel the good ones, wouldn't that be great?" In my effort not to feel the loneliness, pain, and frustration in my life, I gradually went numb. Unfortunately that numbness didn't allow me to feel any of life, even the joyful moments. Though I didn't understand it at the time, I was depressed. One somewhat bright spot in my day was eating. Consequently I did too much of it.

When I was fifteen, I went on a camping trip across the country, which changed my life. We lived outside for two months, in some of the most spectacular national parks this land has to offer. I came to a deep sense of humans in relation to the natural world … on *its* terms. When I returned to our apartment in the city, I realized that modern civilization wasn't all it was cracked up to be. We humans didn't realize that nature was the foundation that everything we did had to be built on. We'd been building a house of cards on the wrong foundation, and we were adding more cards all the time. It seemed to me the cards were bound to fall.

Another way to say this is that one of humanity's great shifts was going to happen sooner rather than later. In my mind I called this great transition "When the Shit Hits the Fan." Later that's what my kids also called it. Since then I've learned the more refined term: "Earth Changes." I see my major task in this life as helping to make that transformation as graceful as possible—or, more straight-forwardly, to minimize the disaster as much as possible. This will require building a new, sustainable infrastructure—not a house of cards—in all facets of life: agriculture, energy, housing, politics, economics, and spirituality. This infrastructure will be built on the foundation of the natural world rather than human imaginings. We will work consciously with the natural world, as is our capacity and destiny as human beings. This is a "Prodigal Son" moment.

This will require us to use the very best of ancient wisdom traditions. Guru Rinpoche, the master who established Buddhism in Tibet, predicted that this transformation will include inner, as well as outer, ways of working with life. At first this transformative approach will act as a transitional safety net when the conventional house of cards finally falls down. Then it will become the new way of life that will carry us forward.

In high school I was fascinated by the mind and how it worked. I watched my classmates for hours, trying to understand them. They began to come to me with their problems. I'd listen sympathetically and try to say something helpful. Many of them jokingly asked me where my psychiatrist's couch was, and told me to send them a bill for my services. Whenever I was actually able to help someone feel better, it made my day.

On that long camping trip when I was fifteen, I remember having brought along a small introductory textbook on Freud, which I read at odd moments, perched in a tree. He provided some fascinating thoughts, but his almost mechanistic view of human beings didn't ring true for me. *Psyche* is the Greek word for soul. Where was the *psyche* in psychology?

By age seventeen I'd discovered Carl Jung and felt most at home with his understandings of the mind. Here I found the psyche in its rightful place, in psychology. Though he called it the "Self," I recognized it as the soul. Since then I've broadened and deepened my understanding of this greater Self, but Jung's input was an important step or two in the right direction.

Meanwhile, as I was exploring psychology, I'd been on a somewhat different track for almost exactly as many years. Although my father was an agnostic acting as a practicing atheist, and my mother said next to nothing on the subject, I was searching: Was there a God or not? I wanted there to be one, but couldn't *see* one. The year after I'd discovered Carl Jung, I actually wrote a song about my spiritual yearning called "Agnostic's Prayer." It really was a heartfelt prayer, asking God to give me a sign—better yet, show Himself to me—so I could see for myself.

Within months I got my sign. While I was visiting my boyfriend and he was doing homework, I was bored. I opened a book

of Baha'i prayers he had lying around, and started reading. For a moment my constantly busy mind shut up and was able to change channels. No doubt helped along by the prayers, it fell into a much more open, clear, quiet state than usual.

My view became vast. I could see and feel the whole universe and its workings, in some way. There was an awareness to it, an enlightened intent that wove itself into reality, from the most subtle levels to the more manifested ones that we all see. When I looked at everyday things from this new point of view, I could see that things weren't solid, as I'd always thought. I could see them, yet could perceive their non-solid nature at the same time. In this same view I saw normally unseen threads of various colors, weaving the tapestry of manifested reality.

This wasn't an abstract treatise on subatomic physics (although physics confirms it); this was my direct experience. My epiphany just seemed to happen, not because of drugs or even meditation techniques. Maybe some people had visions while helped along by chemicals. The only outside help I got was a prayer book, and some quiet time.

Back then, I couldn't fall into this view at will. For a long time afterward, I thought I'd just gotten lucky. Rinpoche later said my realization had emerged through habits of mind from previous lives.

The vast, aware presence infusing it all was probably the most striking part. Yes, I'd gotten my answer, though it didn't look or feel as I'd expected. Now what should I do, wait for scientific proof of God? Even though I couldn't prove it to anyone else, I'd seen the answer for myself. What I'd experienced wasn't the anthropomorphized God I'd usually heard about, no bearded old guy with puppet strings. I decided that, for the sake of convention, I'd call it God. But I knew it to be something quite different from what most people seemed to mean by the word. No wonder that in Jewish tradition there is no attempt to put a name on this … whatever-it-is. My old rabbi, Herman Schaalman, likes to call it "the Mystery."

For a timeless thirty minutes my mind went through a very quick progression: if *this* is the nature of things, my whole understanding of reality had to change. My previous beliefs fell like dominoes, toppling one after the other. One change was a new and undeniable understanding: pursuing something other than a spiritual life was beside the point. I was left with the rhetorical question, "Do I have something *better* to do?" For many months afterward, I "changed channels" at moments during the day, shifted my focus and saw the emptiness/appearance/awareness level of things. It wasn't as full an experience as the epiphany, but I could still sense that things were not as solid as they appeared, and there was a great awareness suffusing—supporting—everything. I could change channels any time I stopped and put my mind to it. Even years afterward I'd change channels, just to see if that reality were still true. It always was. It always is.

Since this truth did seem most important, I began my spiritual quest in earnest … with disappointing results for about twenty-five years.

My two years at college were a great feast of learning, most of which happened outside the classroom. For a young adult, it was a great soup to marinate in, and a formative experience.

Maybe because the weather was dependably terrible, we worked and studied long hours. Still, it was often the conversations and spontaneous teaching we gave each other that most captivated me. I was exposed to Tai Chi, yoga, and organic gardening. I read Ram Dass's *Be Here Now*, which spoke to me, as nothing else had, of my Big Epiphany, not to mention my ongoing experience of the non-solidity of matter: that everything was really made of awareness, or thought.

Toward the end of that first fateful half hour (my epiphany), I had thought, "Now it feels like everything has changed. What shall

I *DO*?" The answer came immediately. "Learn more about this. Pursue a spiritual path."

But HOW does one pursue a spiritual path? I was already taking a course on world religions. I then took a more in-depth course on Taoism, which very much appealed to me. However, I didn't know how to find a Taoist master in No Place, Ohio.

I decided to pursue the life I felt I'd been destined to live, and hoped the wisdom would be available as I went.

No Longer a Child, Not Yet a Buddhist

I didn't make that easy. Since my destiny was to be in the country, and I felt finished with college, I left after my sophomore year. I'd steeped long enough in the campus intellectual marinade, and the course work wasn't going in the direction my mind was going in. I found out about a Theosophical group living and farming in the hills of southwest Wisconsin, so I put my dog and my possessions into my Pinto and drove there.

As it turned out, the members of this group were no longer studying Theosophy, but they certainly were farming. Since they had almost every farm animal you'd expect to see, as well as a big garden, I learned a whole lot. It's also where I met my future husband, the father of my three children.

Though I was involved in almost every part of the operation, Matt and I fell into taking care of the growing goat herd, and were part of the unkempt crew who proudly founded our country's first goat cheese cooperative. After our stint on the farm, Matt spent almost two years working at the little factory that produced the cheese.

After we left the farm, we decided to practice meditation. I still felt there was nothing better or more important to do than to pursue spiritual understanding and development. But there were no teachers in that remote, conservative community, and I was tending my growing family and homestead. After a few years, some of us spiritually aspiring back-to-the-landers started a weekly meditation group. None of us knew what we were doing, so we studied books together, discussed a passage once a week, and finished up with twenty minutes of silence, which we hoped was meditation. We were the blind leading the blind.

Every night Matt and I would sit for fifteen to twenty minutes, after putting the kids to bed. We would try to calm our minds and not have thoughts. Although my mind did calm down, relatively, I certainly wasn't free of thoughts. My focus wasn't turned outward as it normally was, but inward. This shift allowed me to hear that "still, small voice" quietly bubbling up from time to time. Finally, I was there to notice. In a subtle way, it made a huge difference in my life. Coming to myself once a day allowed me to come from a deeper, truer place as I went about my busy life, helping me to stay on track. As I made thousands of tiny decisions each day, I made them a bit more from *that* place.

However, I didn't really notice this was happening. It was

subtle, and the effect increased ever so slowly over the years. I got used to it after a while and couldn't perceive my progress. One day I decided that, since I couldn't get my mind to stop (a typical mistaken Western notion of meditation), and I wasn't getting any instructions for improving this, I might as well stop my paltry attempts altogether. I wasn't doing myself any good and was just wasting time. "Like sitting in a doctor's waiting room or something," I thought. So I really did stop, for about five years.

Eventually—inevitably, as it turns out—my marriage with Matt came to an end. The rightness of marrying him had been so clear; I was surprised when the rightness of ending the marriage made itself equally clear. I did a divination from the *I Ching*, as I'd done with important decisions since I'd bought the book at age thirteen. As if the passage were speaking to me, it basically said, "It *was* right then, and now it's right to leave." I moved to the college town nearby, and went back to school. Later I finished my bachelor's degree and completed an M.A. in Counseling Psychology from a non-residential program. My emphasis was Jungian studies, but I also studied Gestalt and general psychoses.

Amidst all this, I realized one day that my life was totally off track.

Here I was in a brief second marriage, having moved to another city. I was married to someone who was not the right match for me, living in the wrong place, doing the wrong things. It finally became clear, and I knew it, in my heart, in my gut. Those nightly meditations I had given up on five years earlier had actually been making a difference after all, but I hadn't realized it. Just by not having to respond to things outside myself, I had been able to make room for my "still, small voice." And for that brief time, I was there to listen. I finally understood that without those daily moments of respite and clarity, I had made thousands of daily decisions over the past years that had directed, or misdirected, the course of my life.

I took action, both outwardly and inwardly. I moved and took up daily meditation again, this time *promising* myself I'd find a teacher and really follow a course of study and practice properly. "Why reinvent the wheel?" I thought. If you want to get really good at piano, it helps to take lessons from a good piano teacher. Why would it be different for this training?

Every day during my session I'd sound a note out into the universe, calling my teacher. I was specific. I didn't care so much about the specific religion, but the teacher had to be utterly honest, not after my body, really knowledgable, and highly accomplished as a practitioner. It would be several years before my teacher would appear on my doorstep. Literally.

In the meantime, my quest continued. While I was still married to Matt, I had done an apprenticeship in acupressure and set up a small practice. It became clear over the three years of my practice that people's minds were often causing the symptoms in their bodies. That led me back to the area I'd always loved—psychology. Long ago I'd read Jung's autobiography and had dreamed of being a Jungian analyst. That dream returned, with a new, clearer intention. No prospect was more deeply satisfying to me than helping others (and myself) to be better, happier people.

About twenty years after that adolescent dream first stirred, I decided to get some credentials for all this. More than that, if I actually wanted to be a psychotherapist, which I did, I felt I needed to really know what I was doing before people entrusted me with their minds. Though I found I didn't want a Jungian analyst's diploma, I did proceed to get a master's degree in Counseling Psychology that focused heavily on Jung—then the non-credentialed equivalent of another master's degree. I eventually opened my own practice.

I was unbelievably lucky in the quality of the teachers and the skillful techniques I had encountered in my long years of training. Most students of Western psychology aren't so fortunate. Probably because it's such a new field in our culture, there's a whole lot of bad psychology being taught and practiced out there. Because of the excellent training I'd had, I was able to practice some decent psychology, and my clients reported feeling better. Still, I felt the methods were slow, inefficient, and unevenly effective.

I Meet the Buddha on the Path

Not long after I moved to Boulder, Colorado, a haven for anything New Age or spiritual, I went about tasting from the spiritual smorgasbord. One method that attracted me was Vipassana, Insight Meditation. This is from the Theravada, or School of the Elders, branch of Buddhism, since it was the first set of methods the Buddha taught. Vipassana is still practiced widely in Burma and Thailand. My instructors, Sharon Salzberg and Joseph Goldstein, studied it in both places for years. I found it helpful that they had learned from a genuine master, steeped in an unbroken lineage. Their teaching was so much more grounded than the New Age workshops that proliferated around me. I found it at least as helpful that these instructors were Americans themselves. They could translate not only the words, but the methods, into something this American could relate to.

Shortly after earning my master's degree, I took a year-and-a half-long course in psychotherapy, taught by Zen meditation teachers. One of these instructors was an ordained Zen nun; one of the students was an American Zen *roshi*, or abbot. The training they offered focused on body-centered and Gestalt modalities, but the overall context was Buddhist. We meditated at the start of each training day. The roshi combined forces with the teachers and put on a ten-day retreat, with equal parts Zen practice and psychotherapy.

I had another, even deeper epiphany.

Yet I was still not satisfied with Zen. How was I to get to enlightenment just by quieting my mind and answering koans? Stylistically, it was also too martial and sparse for me. Some people love Zen, but I was looking for more of a counterpart to the Western methods of understanding the workings of the mind, such as Jungian psychology. I wanted an approach that used the tendencies of the mind in a full and varied way to help it better itself.

My Root Lama: Tulku Sangak Rinpoche

FIRST MEETING

When I first met Tulku Sangak Rinpoche, I wasn't expecting to. In fact, I wasn't expecting to meet anyone.

It was my first solitary retreat, for ten days in the desert outside Santa Fe, in the casita next to Sherab's. Sherab was the American lama who had first introduced me to Vajrayana, and he gave me instruction and guidance on this, my first foray into retreat. I was working on the first two sections of the Preliminary Practices—the *Ngöndro*—a set of five foundational Vajrayana practices. I'd made great progress on the second one in particular, which mainly focuses on expanding our capacity for compassion. I would soon be ready for the third section, which focuses on clearing away our faults and karma.

Just as I was finishing retreat, about thirty people gathered, to be with a rinpoche—a high lama—who appeared at this house in the middle of the desert. I hadn't been aware of this program that Sherab had planned. The high lama was going to give an "empowerment," an initiation which would open their minds to the practice that was to be taught, and connect them to it in a deep way. What practice might that be? The very next one I was going to do! Who was this lama? Tulku Sangak Rinpoche, whom I'd never heard of. I thought, "Oh, I might as well go to it—I'm already here and my retreat just finished, so I have the time."

After the empowerment, I came for a personal interview with Rinpoche. Since he didn't know a word of English, and at the time I didn't know a word of Tibetan, we needed a translator. It just happened to be Sangye Khandro, a leading translator in the West, who had almost never translated for Rinpoche.

Rinpoche was medium height and wiry, with dark, weathered skin. Somehow the patterns of his wrinkles made beautiful designs. He seemed middle-aged, but it was impossible to tell how old he really was. When he smiled, he showed big white teeth, and the weathered skin crinkled around his eyes in the most appealing shapes. His smiles were infectious. Luckily they came almost constantly, in waves, sometimes tiny, sometimes huge, accompanied by a surprisingly high-pitched laugh that tickled me from the inside so that I had to laugh too. And this was before the translation of what he said.

Contrary to many Western notions about enlightened Asian masters, Rinpoche hardly stayed still. Sometimes he doodled with a pencil and paper while waiting for the translations back and forth. Sometimes he lightly jumped up and paced around the room. Wherever he went, he left trails of graceful line drawings of lotuses, clouds, calligraphy, and other images. His fine-boned hands made the most lovely gestures that had a grace about them that wasn't at all like Western men's, yet wasn't in the least effeminate. His voice was low and kind of froggy, occasionally leaping into falsetto to emphasize a word here or there. I've since noticed that the Dalai Lama and many other Tibetan men use this falsetto for emphasis as well.

I thought of a question for which I wanted a clear, definitive answer. Many, if not most, of the Buddhists in the world are vegetarian. If Tibetans are devout Buddhists, with compassion for *all* beings, why do most of them eat meat? I was eating mostly vegetarian at the time, and was a lifelong animal lover, so it was important to me and I couldn't make sense of this. What about the karma involved for the one eating the meat?

I put the question to him. He said, "If we actually kill an animal ourselves, it holds the most serious karmic consequences for us. It's murder, of course. If we do this repeatedly, we develop a habit of killing, which will follow us, along with the karmic seeds, into future lives. The next worst thing is if we choose a particular animal and ask that it be killed for us to eat." At that point I thought of restaurants that offer to kill the lobster of your choice, from a huge aquarium. I could see his points for both of these examples. Then he went on. "It's much better if we just go to the store and pick up any package of meat and buy it." That didn't make much sense to me.

"Wait, but how does that work karmically, Rinpoche? We're still paying money that goes back to the butcher who did the killing. It's indirect, but it still gets there. This encourages him and other butchers to keep on killing animals for a living. We're voting with our dollars for the killing of animals. In America we have laws against paying someone else to kill a person for us. Isn't this a close relative of that? True, we haven't chosen a specific animal, but aren't we stepping into other, additional karmic territory when we encourage someone else to murder by paying them to do so? And by the way, what about the karma we now have with the butchers?"

After some back and forth on this point, Rinpoche said, "Of

course, the very best is to give up meat altogether. A few great masters in exile don't eat meat, and they don't allow their students to either. Another practice we traditionally do in Tibet, to make the situation a little better, is to wait until the butcher has offered the meat to two other people. The thought is that if the animal has already died, then we're simply eating the meat before the bugs get it." He and I came to agreement that not eating meat was optimal, but barring that, the more distance between the eater and the killing, the better.

Our short, lively discussion took a few loops and bends along its course, but essentially that was what we discussed in the landmark interview. Then it was over. I didn't think much about it, except for some more about Tibetans and meat. For example, since they live in a very extreme and challenging environment, and almost the only things that grow there are trees (mostly conifers) and grass, they don't have a lot of dietary options. Their only real options are to eat the grass and the grass-eaters. Toasted barley flour is a staple there, so that would be a small part of the grass. But without four stomachs, they wouldn't be able to get all their nutrition from grass, especially for withstanding the rigors of the high Himalayas; and this without indoor heat. As a practical matter, how could such an environment support a human population if they didn't eat the grass-eaters?

Shortly after that conversation, I had to give up vegetarianism because of increasingly serious health problems. I still don't feel fully resolved on this issue, even though His Holiness the Dalai Lama has also had to go back to eating meat.

In all of this pondering, the most obvious, striking point never occurred to me. This lama, who had just dropped in from nowhere to this out-of-the-way place, happened to be giving a lineage transmission and introduction to the very next practice I was about to start doing … *and I didn't get that he was the teacher I'd been praying for!*

THE SECOND MEETING: RECOGNITION

The next time I saw Rinpoche he came to my *house*. For two weeks. With one of the world's best translators, Chökyi Nyima (Richard Barron), who at the time never did that sort of event.

Yes, I did finally get a clue, but slowly.

We *thought* that Rinpoche was coming because Sherab no longer lived at the house near Santa Fe and needed to get some teachings from Rinpoche. At the time Sherab was staying in a cramped apartment with two other people. Would I mind hosting him, Rinpoche, and Chökyi while he got Dzogchen teachings, the highest in Vajrayana, for a couple of weeks? Sure, why not?

Another sign I had totally missed at the time was from a dinner I'd had two years earlier with Ram Dass.* I was a longtime fan, and I'd asked him which meditation might be best for me to pursue. He uttered one strange word: *Dzogchen*. Now, here was Sherab coming to my home to study Dzogchen from one of the world's foremost Dzogchen lamas, and I'd totally forgotten Ram Dass's advice!

Sherab said I could sit in on the teachings. This didn't make sense to me. I was doing Ngöndro, the very beginning stage of Vajrayana; Dzogchen was the very highest level. Why would I plop down into these high-level teachings at this point? Sherab kept assuring me it didn't matter, but I wasn't convinced. It seemed to me that it could cause problems for me and the others there.

---

* Ram Dass, a.k.a. Richard Alpert, wrote *Be Here Now,* after having studied yogic mind training in India. This had a huge cultural effect on many, especially in the 1970s. He continues to be a much-read and listened-to voice on spirituality for Westerners.

As the time drew closer, I became more concerned. Then something else happened. I found out that Sherab had been turning other people away from this teaching, telling them that *I* had pronounced it a "closed retreat." This seemed totally against the order of things. Wouldn't that be up to the lama doing the teaching? The other issue was that, well, Sherab had just made that up. Since he had told me that for Dzogchen teachings, the connections between participants had to be utterly clean, I became really concerned about the convergence of these issues leading up to the retreat. I called Rinpoche. Fortunately Chökyi, the translator, "happened" to be on hand. Through him, I expressed my concerns to Rinpoche about both the appropriateness of my sitting in and Sherab's telling people that I'd declared it a closed retreat. I felt that both matters were up to Rinpoche as the teacher.

Rinpoche said that he saw my concern as a very good sign, and that I was right to call. He went on to say that the heart of the matter was my motivation, and he could see that my motivation was pure. For that reason, he knew that everything would play out well. He would start by giving some Ngöndro teachings; then we would just see how it went. That was all he expressed, yet somehow I hung up with all of my concerns laid to rest. I felt happy and ready for the retreat.

Just before he arrived, Sherab gave me a little advice. He said, "I know you love to ask questions and hammer out points. Your questions and thinking are all great, and I really appreciate it, but this is a rinpoche—a high lama. Tibetans find it disrespectful to ask a lot of questions."

"Really?" I exclaimed, recalling the questions I had showered Rinpoche with, and our lively debate during our first meeting. What he was saying didn't fit with my experience of Rinpoche. Besides, there was a practical need here. "But ... what if I need to know the *answer*?"

"Just don't ask too many questions."

I found this to be an impossible conundrum. "But how will I find out the answer? Why is he coming here if I can't find things out from him? What's disrespectful about asking a question?" I asked, my questions coming out in a torrent. His admonition to ask no questions only stimulated more questions!

The first day we opened with a *tsok*, or gathering. This ceremonial feast usually lasts about two hours and involves a constant

stream of melodious chanting in Tibetan, punctuated by drums and bells. Every so often Sherab, who was assisting, would walk in or out, carrying symbolic cakes which had been sculpted into inscrutable shapes. Luckily, toward the end we got to stop and eat the feast that had been offered and blessed during the ceremony.

We could have a bit of conversation, thanks to the translator. Then there were concluding prayers to finish it off.

Since at that time I knew absolutely no Tibetan, nor anything about such ceremonies, I was at a loss. Fortunately the constant chant was a beautiful, intricate melody. It was sometimes alternated with another, simpler one. As one looking at the prospect of becoming a Vajrayana practitioner, I wasn't sure how I would do with all the pomp and circumstance. I'd been drawn to Vajrayana by the effective mind-training methods. I didn't see what all this two-hour ceremony had to do with that.

It was years before I would learn that it was all a group meditation, guided by the liturgy, with visualizations that, in refined archetypal language, honored the land guardians, brought forth various aspects of my own Buddha Nature, made extensive use of archetypes, and worked with emotions and energies in

highly refined ways. When I say "highly refined," I mean that these methods of guiding the mind to a more enlightened state have been developed and distilled over thousands of years, with millions of people, to achieve their desired effect. The process, if done consciously, can be quite powerful, with surprising effects. Who knew?

At last we settled down for the first session of teachings. According to plan, Rinpoche held forth on the first stages of the Ngöndro, or Preliminary Practices, which I had already gotten a good start on. He was constantly bringing forth fascinating and profound levels of understanding.

These understandings rang true for me.

I was writing notes furiously. After he had held forth on the "Bodhicitta training" section for a while, he opened it up for questions. I looked at Sherab. He gave a slight nod. I was at least permitted one question.

"Rinpoche, you've just told us that in practicing the highest form of Bodhicitta, we put others' needs before ours, like a shepherd. But you've also said we need to become enlightened first before we can really help sentient beings to break free of Samsara. Aren't there times when it's like the oxygen mask on an airplane? Parents are told to put their *own* mask on first, not out of self-interest, but *so that* they can best help their child. What are we to do in the case of enlightenment ourselves? When do we work to directly benefit others, and when do we work directly on our own minds, even if the ultimate altruistic goal is the same?"

Rinpoche seemed to wake up, and leaned forward. He talked in a very energetic, animated way for some time. Then Chökyi translated: "We do need to pursue enlightenment in order to be of any use in helping other Samsaric beings. How can we help a drowning person if we can't swim ourselves?" (This made sense to me. When I studied Junior Life Saving, the instructors began with that very point, and trained us accordingly.) We pursue our own enlightenment *in order* to help others. This is why in Mahayana, or Great Vehicle, Buddhism, we begin all of our practice sessions, ceremonies, and teachings by arousing Bodhicitta.* We bring forward in our minds what's known as the Two Purposes: enlightenment for self and others. We're doing this practice on behalf of all sentient beings, even in the Dharma activity, such as study and practice.

But the benefit continues. Because of the training we do, we're far more masterful at helping others during the course of the day. We're less likely to fall into anger, protect our own projects at the expense of others', get distracted, and so on. If we carry

---

* In Sanskrit, *Bodhicitta* means "heart/mind of awakening." This awakened heart/mind feels our connection to all beings, therefore their joy and pain.

this desire to serve others on their path of enlightenment (whether they're consciously pursuing it or not), we then bring forth our own Buddha Nature, which in turn serves to help our own enlightenment process. This then translates into clearer seeing (through a cleaner windshield) and better meditation. These support each other, and everyone, you and they, moves forward, just as a shepherd moves forward with the flock. He continued leaning forward, clearly fully engaged. He was having fun; I was sure of it. For all I could tell, he liked answering questions *best of all*. "Do you have any more questions?" he queried.

It just so happened I did. I'd been writing them in the margins as Rinpoche was going along. But I had a different question I had to ask first, to clear the air. "I've been told that asking questions of a high lama such as you is disrespectful. Is that true?"

Rinpoche looked perplexed, then went on for longer than I expected, ending by laughing at his own joke. I experienced delayed gratification, waiting for the translator to relay all this to me.

"How will you learn if you don't ask questions? Also it will be impossible for me to know where your understanding is if I don't hear your questions. When I first began teaching the nuns, I would lecture awhile, then ask for questions. The nuns were trained to be VERY humble in general, particularly with men, and much more so with a rinpoche." (Here was a Tibetan cultural tendency. Later, at the monastery, when a man they didn't know very well was in the room, I rarely heard them speak.) "They would just titter behind their hands, too shy to speak. This went on for a few rounds, until I said, 'This isn't going to work. If I don't hear your questions, I don't know how you're doing, what you understand and what you don't, HOW you understand, and how your mind works. Next time I open it up for questions, if you don't ask me, *I'll ask each of you!*'" (That's when Rinpoche had laughed!) "The nuns began asking questions, and now they're quite used to it, along with debate and discussion. They're coming along quite well."

I continued with my list. Rinpoche and I were fully engaged, and the electricity was palpable. Chökyi, the translator, was like an open door, allowing the ideas to flow back and forth effortlessly between languages, almost as though we were speaking the same language. The knowledge, clarity, and depth of Rinpoche's answers electrified me. Years later, Rinpoche told me that he was pleased with the way my mind was working with the material. As a modern American, this was my first experience of the master-student relationship which has been extensively written about for centuries in some form or another, in all of Asia, and even ancient Greece.

Though my rabbi was truly wise and kind, and he spoke with knowledge, clarity, and depth, I had never experienced the roaring torrent of the pursuit of truth between two people in quite this way before. I've since had the chance to discuss and debate with Rabbi Schaalman, and the process did feel very similar. Surprisingly, though, I felt less of a recognition—a ringing true—with some of the Jewish theological points than I had with the Buddhist ones.

Back in my living room with Rinpoche that fateful day, the torrent of our questions, answers, and discussion was tumbling along with grace and power, bouncing over the terrain as it followed its natural path. Chökyi, with his scintillating mind and love of the subject, was flowing right along with us. When it was over, I'd no idea how much time had passed. It felt like five minutes; I think it was about an hour. We were all beaming, and though Chökyi must have been tired from the rigors of translating, we felt deeply invigorated.

It was love at first question.

Rinpoche's teachings continued, going deeper all the while. He moved into the Dzogchen portion, allowing me to come along on the first steps, while he carefully watched how I interacted with the material. He held forth for a bit on the true nature of reality, then sent us off with a question to ponder in silence on our own. We were to write notes and then report back to Rinpoche. We went through several rounds of this process. Well, I would write notes. Lots of them.

When we gathered again, he asked us what conclusions we'd come to, and how we'd gotten there. Sherab uttered a vague sentence, then fell into silence. We were all quiet, waiting. Nothing. Rinpoche shrugged and turned to me.

You'll be surprised to know that I had more than a page, densely packed with notes. This happened more than once. I explained them all to Rinpoche. He occasionally stopped me and elucidated a point, but he mostly listened. I had no idea if I was sounding like a blithering idiot. I was sure I'd gone on too long, and was hoping I wasn't TOO far off track. When I'd finished, Rinpoche laughed and said something to Chökyi. This didn't reassure me.

As it turned out, he was quite pleased and he was laughing with delight. I'd stumbled upon the general direction he'd hoped for! He then clarified a few points, which did make much more sense to me once he'd honed them. His points were fascinating, and opened up my understanding of reality.

Then he surprised me. He said, "I'll make a statement, you pick a side, and let's debate." I think my mouth must have dropped open. That's exactly what my dad used to say at the dinner table, to signal the start of our nightly debates! These were loads of fun, with familial debaters occasionally jumping up to consult the encyclopedia to support a point. We three kids were in hot pursuit of Dad, who would make leaps and dives in logic, sometimes leading us by the nose, only to tap us from behind and win his point. Every once in a while we'd have him cornered, and it was time for him to admit we were right. But his pride wouldn't quite allow him to give in to his kids. So we had no choice: an all-out napkin fight would ensue, fairly athletic, accompanied by raucous laughter. Mom would cover her face, warning, "Look out for my contact lenses! My contacts, my contacts!" This was often the grand finale to our dinners.

Needless to say, I was ready for the debate with Rinpoche. I have no idea if my points were worth anything in the Dzogchen context, but Rinpoche and I were off and running. We were having a grand time, and I was learning a mile a minute. Alas, not having had the benefit of my childhood dinner table, Sherab sat mute. I was letting it all hang out: my ignorance and knowledge, and of course my enthusiasm for the topic. Sherab seemed to be holding it all in. I couldn't tell what was happening inside my dear friend. Was he horrified at my uppitiness? Surprised at the whole turn of events? Frustrated that he couldn't jump in? Surely he wasn't lost … or was he? I just couldn't read his unmoving face. Afterward I felt concerned for him.

Later I heard him teaching his little Sangha in the Bay Area, beautifully weaving in the Dzogchen understandings Rinpoche had brought us. Everything had no doubt registered, but both his culture and his own personality were vastly different from mine. My personality and cultural tendencies certainly limit me in some frustrating ways, but I was sad that Sherab's own tendencies didn't allow Rinpoche to see how much he'd understood after all. They never did connect very strongly, probably because of destiny as much as anything else, and Sherab has since moved on.

Back at the seminal Dzogchen retreat, the teachings progressed apace. One night Chökyi left to visit some friends. Sherab withdrew to his room for the duration.

When Chökyi walked out, the translation door instantly slammed shut. We didn't have a word in common. My teenage daughter Anna, Rinpoche, and I looked at each other. Now what? Rinpoche got the goofiest look on his face, plopped a hat on at a crazy angle, and pranced around, laughing his high-pitched laugh. He was totally *silly*. Anna and I cracked up. I grabbed Sherab's size 14 wide shoes and clomped around, my toothpick ankles looking particularly ridiculous sticking out of them. Rinpoche threw his head back, laughing. Then we were arm wrestling. Then an uproarious tickle fight.

Later, Rinpoche watched, fascinated, as I cooked up our dinner. Between prison and monasteries, I guessed that he'd never learned to cook a thing. The next morning I found this to be true. He sheepishly asked me to show him how to light the stove burner, so he could make his early morning tea.

It also occurred to Anna and me that as a *tulku* (high, reincarnated lama), maybe he'd rarely had this kind of silly, irreverent, slapstick interaction with people. This turned out to be mostly true as well, except for some times, especially earlier in his life, when he was with fellow tulkus. As the head of a lineage, now mostly presiding over his own monastery, he didn't get the chance often. That night the time flew by as we all partied down.

A different kind of bonding can happen outside the teaching arena—beyond words as well. I learned still more about Rinpoche that evening. His obsession for learning, whether fine points about a Dharma text or how a gas stove works, knows no bounds. You can be sure he'll spend time contemplating the inscrutable English writing (Light, Off, Hi, Lo) on the knobs. He doesn't identify with one persona or another. He's equally believable, equally comfortable—equally himself—whether wearing the lineage lama crown while teaching thousands of devout followers, or losing an arm-wrestling match and collapsing into falsetto giggles. He never forgets his true essence, which can take any form.

Toward the end of the teachings, I began asking him questions about my college epiphany that no one had been able to explain. I can't go into detail here because you would first need to have had Dzogchen empowerments and teachings. Much of the Dzogchen knowledge is closely guarded, partly so that the practitioner hears the teachings freshly when their mind has been made thoroughly ready. Then they can fall into seeing/experiencing things as they naturally are. What I want to tell you and *can* tell you here is that when I heard his answers, they instantly rang true. This was the first time in my life that had happened.

I didn't register it consciously at the moment, but I had already come to know that he was my lama.

At that time I was in the editing phase of a book I'd written, which included traditional stories of feminine journeys, with female protagonists displaying distinctly feminine strengths. Instead of killing dragons to save their beloveds, they wielded the power of loving connection, endurance, and other feminine traits. I wanted both boys and girls to be fed these images so that they would have those models to follow in their own lives. A central thought of mine was that we all need to balance the masculine and feminine principles, using the best of both.

One night during the retreat, Rinpoche mentioned that he was doing research for a book he wanted to write on female *mahasiddhas*—highly realized beings. He wanted to provide models for Tibetans, especially women, so they would believe that they too could reach enlightenment. Imagine my surprise and delight! Later in the conversation he mentioned that he wanted to call his new nonprofit *Ewam*, the Sanskrit word meaning "the union of the realized masculine and feminine principles." At that moment there was a ratification in my head, confirming what I'd already come to know. Inside, in celebration of the obvious, I rejoiced, "This is the lama for me!"

As we waited together for his plane, he played with the turquoise *mala* he'd been fiddling with almost constantly through-out the teachings. This was the mala that he'd been praying with and handling during his waking hours, for the year since Sherab had given it to him. As he tossed it lightly back and forth between his hands, I had this odd idea that he was going to give it to me. I thought, "Oh, how conceited!" They announced that it was time to board. Suddenly, deliberately, he pressed the mala into my hand and lightly skipped off to the plane. I stood there, stunned. After some time my legs moved, but I was still stunned.

A primary relationship had begun, the likes of which I'd never heard about, much less experienced. It was more profound and intimate than a romantic one, more enduring than familial ones in some ways, more primary in some ways than any I'd known. It took time to develop fully—in this lifetime anyway—but develop it did. This sort of experience was hardly a novelty in Asia, but to me it was entirely uncharted territory of the heart.

As Rinpoche knew from the beginning and I came to know much later, our relationship had begun lifetimes ago, and will no doubt go on into future ones. Who knows how many times he's patiently shown me the nature of my mind, of reality, and the rela-tionship between the two? To this day our connection continually

deepens. And as my capacity of mind has grown, I've been able to see Rinpoche's vast, wise mind more and more fully. As a natural result, my love for and devotion to him have grown even richer and more profound.

When I first had teachings from Rinpoche, he was the only one in all my life who could thoroughly explain to me, in a way that rang true, all that I'd seen in that epiphany so long ago. He has since gone on to teach me methods that can bring that same level of seeing and more, every time I meditate! Even in between. Not only that, I'm far happier, ongoing, than I was before.

It didn't happen overnight, and it didn't happen without effort. I'm also definitely not finished yet, though it's been nearly two decades and I've spent two to three months out of most of those years in solitary, strict practice retreat. How realistic is it to expect enlightenment in ten easy lessons? If we've been wandering around Samsara for endless lifetimes since "beginningless time," getting all the more ingrained and entangled in wrong ways of seeing and doing, it's going to take a little while to turn ourselves around.

Fortunately this path has its rewards along the way—some lofty, some more mundane. On a very practical level, right after I'd had those first teachings with Rinpoche I was able to give up smoking … *through lack of interest!* Have you ever heard of that? I hadn't. Because he'd helped me connect so well with the practices, they were so satisfying on every level—even a gut level—that I actually forgot to smoke.

There was much I'd turned to—taken refuge in—that I was gradually able to loosen my grip on as I went along, including angry words and behavior. I'm not perfect, but I'm much improved and much happier. As I've said, the level of awareness I can reach in my daily meditation meets and can even surpass my first epiphany. For now, I'll take that.

The Young Tulku Sangak Rinpoche's Footprint in the Rock

WHY TULKU SANGAK RINPOCHE BOTHERED

🌸 *Background*

The lama I was so fortunate to meet many years ago is from a family that served the community, in both spirituality and medicine, as the equivalent to Native American medicine people, since before Buddhism came to Tibet. Once they accepted Buddhism, they joined the great Nyingma Lineage, first established when Guru Rinpoche transformed Tibet into a Buddhist country in the ninth century A.C.E. (After the Common Era). Their own family lineage, the Namchak (Meteorite) Lineage, is a comparatively short and direct one. Still, as with many smaller lineages, it's within the larger Nyingma Lineage.

One day when Tulku Sangak Rinpoche was just old enough to run around—still a toddler—he was playing on the hillside with his little friends. The weather was warm, and they were barefoot. As they were running up the hill, he found he could easily sink his foot into the bare rock, leaving a clear imprint, as though it were soft mud. Actually the rock was particularly hard in that area. The other children noticed the imprint and drew their breath in

51

amazement. They ran to tell the adults nearby. Everyone whispered that this must be a great reincarnated lama—a *tulku*!

As word quickly spread, a woman from another lineage became unhappy. When she thought no one was looking, she went to that hillside and tried to chisel out the clear footprint. The stone was so hard that after hours of work she had managed to chisel only two tiny places from the middle of the imprint. She became nervous, gave up the pursuit, and left. Of course, in such a small community, everyone found out about her efforts.

As you can see, the imprint of the little toes is very clear, as is the heel. In the middle are the two little black holes that the lady managed to chisel out.

When Tulku Sangak Rinpoche was about three years old and just barely able to put simple sentences together, his parents told him he would be the keeper of their family lineage. He answered, "No, I'm the tulku (reincarnated lama) of the *Gochen* Monasteries" —a group of monasteries in the Namchak Lineage and in the same province, but not right where they lived. His parents were startled, and not entirely pleased. They wanted him to live in their ancestral home-cum-monastery and take care of the lineage *there*. They quickly hushed him: "Shhh. Don't tell anybody."

Soon after, they were walking down the streets of town and came upon a high lama with the usual sign—an ornamental knob with a tassel hanging from the bridle of his horse. This lama's name was Dzigar Kongtrül Rinpoche. He was another rinpoche (high lama), who had been a dear friend of my lama, Tulku Sangak Rinpoche, in his own previous incarnation. (Since that meeting, Dzigar Kongtrül passed away, then reincarnated himself, and now lives in Colorado. Even in this life he is still called Dzigar Kongtrül Rinpoche.) When these two rinpoches met that day long ago, on that street in Tibet, the tiny Sangak Rinpoche (my lama) pointed to the ornament and called out, "Hey, that's MINE!" At first Dzigar Kongtrül paid no attention. The tiny Rinpoche insisted louder and

louder, saying, "I gave it to you, now give it BACK!" Finally Kongtrül Rinpoche got off his horse and approached the toddler. He looked at him closely, calculated his age, and thought, "He really could be my old friend, the Gochen Tulku, who passed away about four years ago."

Shortly before he died, the Gochen Tulku had given that tassel to his good friend Kongtrül Rinpoche, asking him to keep it until he returned. The lama asked the little boy several questions. Being just under three years old, he forgot his parents' admonishments and answered truthfully. He was, indeed, the Gochen Tulku. Now everyone on the street knew it; there was no hiding it.

Shortly after, the famous Jamyang Khyentse Chökyi Lodrö the Great did a divination and announced that this remarkable little child was indeed the new incarnation of the Gochen Tulku. He went on to list his parents by name, and his hometown. He then sent a horse for the boy. Oh well; the parents relented.

From a very young age, Rinpoche was groomed to be the holder of the Namchak Lineage. He also holds the Longchen Nyingtik, Chetsün Nyingtik, and Mindröling Lineages, among others.

His training was not as it had been for his other six lives as the lineage-holding lama of the Gochen Monasteries, though. During the Chinese Cultural Revolution, the monasteries were destroyed, and, as you know, he was thrown into prison at the age of fourteen. During that tumultuous time, the Chinese government tried to stamp out all spirituality and religion, which they saw as "the opiate of the people." So they didn't look kindly on spiritual leaders such as Rinpoche, even though he was quite young.

When he was nine, the Chinese had tried to make him do "real work" and sent him with a young shepherd to herd sheep. Being Tibetan, the shepherd found a cave where Rinpoche could hide his books.

Rinpoche continued to study and practice in secret. During their war with India, the Chinese government had called a lot of its troops away to the front, and there was the tumult of the Cultural Revolution inside China to deal with as well. Everyone in Rinpoche's area had been doing their ceremonies secretly in barns, with the windows covered, silencing their bells by wrapping cloth around them. But now, with the Chinese distracted, they got more and more brave about openly practicing Dharma.

Finally, on a holy day, they brought everything out and celebrated a beautiful, grand ceremony, on the top of a hill. Unfortunately, the troops were just coming back after the war. Someone must have told them about the ceremony, and they had a big trial. Everyone who had been in the ceremony tried to protect Rinpoche, their lineage holder, insisting it was their doing, not his. Rinpoche said that he was the leader, and he was responsible—this, at age fourteen.

As they often did with Tibetan spiritual leaders, the Chinese tried to discredit him. They knew that he had taken a vow not to kill any being, so they gave him an ultimatum. They would gather the townspeople the next day, and either he would kill a sheep in front of them all or the soldiers would kill him. That night he lay awake, trying out different strategies and scenarios in his head. He didn't have a lot of good options. Finally he came up with the best plan he could think of.

The next day they brought him to the middle of town, where they had gathered a throng of villagers. A villager in front of him was holding the bound sheep. The guard, a Tibetan working for the Chinese, ordered him to kill the sheep. It was often the Tibetans who had gone over to the Chinese who were the harshest on their fellow Tibetans—a common irony wherever one people has conquered another. But in this case, Rinpoche planned to use his countryman's antagonism to his advantage.

Rinpoche put his plan into action. He began waving his arms wildly, talking Dharma and screaming out quotes from the scriptures. He was hoping to make the guard so angry that the guard would hit him. At first the guard was just befuddled. As Rinpoche got more and more outrageous, the guard finally became incensed, and gave the young, skinny Rinpoche a wallop that knocked him down.

Then things happened very fast. The villager forced to hold the sheep for this performance "lost control" of it, and the sheep scampered off through the crowd. Now there was no sheep to kill, so the de-morality play was over. And Rinpoche was promptly put in prison.

In Prison, but Not Imprisoned

He remained there for nearly ten years. During most of that time, he couldn't even send his family a letter to let them know he was alive. At first he was kept in a sort of warehouse for prisoners, then later sent to other prisons and made to do hard labor all day. For example, for one stint he had to pull a plow twelve hours a day. Whichever prison he was in, he was always confined with the "worst threats to society"—the other lineage holders, great masters, and scholars of Dharma. He was part of an all-star cast, which, ironically, never would have been gathered together except for his imprisoners' antagonism and fear.

He took full advantage of his situation, studying with many great lamas. He especially studied with one of the greatest lamas of the time, Tulku Orgyen Chemchok, who was key in completely transforming his experience. Rinpoche has said that when he first arrived, even more intolerable than the scant, terrible food, the crowded conditions, or the harsh treatment by the guards was the searing anger in his heart. His outer circumstances were challenging, to say the least, but it was the firebrand of resentment, burning twenty-four hours a day inside his heart, that he found intolerable.

It was when they moved him to a labor camp and worked him like an ox, that he met Tulku Orgyen Chemchok, who had been in permanent retreat in the mountains when the Chinese bound him and brought him to prison. He was working there as a cook.

He asked Rinpoche, "Are you just pretending to do the work, while breaking tools or just making a noise when they're not looking?" He was. "Don't you see? In some lifetime, maybe millions of years ago, you planted the karmic seed that has now ripened into this circumstance. If you didn't still have the traces of that previous action in your mindstream, it would be impossible for you to find yourself in this circumstance. Now that you're here, you could simply do the work to be done, and practice while that karmic result exhausts itself, or you could make more negative karma—plant the seeds for future misery—all the while. Then in some lifetime you'll have to live through that result, too." Rinpoche could see his point.

"Do you realize that, just as your karmic load is lightening from repaying some karmic debt, the guards are taking on an extremely heavy one? If you think about it, they deserve your sincere compassion." True enough. After all, Rinpoche had studied the law of cause and effect, action and result, known as *karma*. *Karma* is a Sanskrit word, literally meaning "action." We have a corollary in the famous Biblical quote, "Ye shall reap what ye sow."

Rinpoche took the tulku's sage advice to heart. He spent every Sunday, when they had a day off from work, helping the tulku, studying, and practicing. He somehow managed to practice a surprising amount in secret, all week. Of course they were forbidden to study Dharma, or even to possess a bit of paper with teachings on it. So the tulku put grease on a flat metal surface, sprinkled sand on it, and wrote crucial bits of the scriptural teachings and practice instructions on the surface. Rinpoche would have to memorize it on the spot; then they would destroy any trace of the writing.

He put the teachings into practice as he did his work, before and after work, at lunch break, in any way he could. He tied many knots in a string, and secretly recited mantras while counting on his string like a rosary, under his sleeve. Soon the burning anger was gone from his heart, he had a much more kind and compassionate view toward his captors, and life was becoming tolerable—more

than tolerable. Gradually, he was actually beginning to feel contentment. Later, while practicing openly outside Tibet, Rinpoche found that all the scriptures and oral explanations, which the tulku had taught him from memory, had been faultless.

Finally Rinpoche experienced something that changed his heart forever. After he had been in prison for years, Tulku Orgyen Chemchok asked him, "How are you collecting food for the pigs?" The prison kept pigs, which the guards and prisoners ate. The prisoners were required to earn daily "credit" for a certain number of pounds of leaves for the pigs, after a long, hard day's work in the woods. The feed truck would come by, and the prisoners would load their amount onto the scale. Not surprisingly, they mostly loaded big branches, rather than leaves, because branches weighed more and were easier to gather. Rinpoche did the same. The tulku said, "Come with me." He took Rinpoche to the pig pen.

There were the pigs, who were meant to forage in the woods, but instead were cooped up in a pen. They had nothing under their feet but all the sticks left over from their feed, covered with the slime of their own filth. They could hardly walk on that surface. There were searching desperately through a fresh load of feed for the few leaves they could actually eat. A sharp pang of deep compassion sprang up in Rinpoche's heart. He burst into tears. These pigs were in prison too—one far worse than his. They were just as powerless to escape as he was. Then, of course, there was the fate awaiting them. After their short life in this excruciating pen, they would be killed. He vowed with all his heart to feed them well, and to convince his prison friends to do the same. They all agreed, and from then on collected only leaves for the pigs.

This was about much more than a few pigs. Rinpoche's heart had completely turned. He had truly taken the Dharma to heart, and into action, living more purely out of compassion for all beings. Finally, he came to feel truly happy, all of this while still in prison. That firebrand of resentment was extinguished—replaced by peace and joy.

Not coincidentally, he had gone from an inner hell-realm experience to that of a pure realm (the Tibetan equivalent of heaven), even though his outer circumstances hadn't changed. The Buddha taught that to live from our small sense of Self (ego, meaning "I" in Latin) is a recipe for misery. To live with a vast sense of Self that includes all sentient beings is a recipe for happiness.

Rinpoche recognized that all the while he was in prison, his karma for that situation was exhausting itself as he followed the tulku's advice and the Buddha's teaching. In his view, it was a sort of work-study program at a monastery with bad food.

Whenever I want to blame outer circumstances, or other people, for my mood, this story helps me put it all into perspective. It also inspires me to have real faith in these methods, with Rinpoche's ability to apply them in "real time" as a sublime example.

After Rinpoche had been in prison for over nine years, Mao Zedong died, the Cultural Revolution along with him. Soon Rinpoche and all the others imprisoned simply for religious leadership were allowed to go.

After he was released, he did a traditional form of traveling retreat for a year. In Lhasa, the capital of Tibet, he met with his lama, Tulku Orgyen Chemchok, who advised him to leave the country. "You need to study with great lamas, and that can't happen here in Tibet, now." So with a companion, another tulku, Rinpoche escaped Tibet.

He arrived in Bhutan and studied under the great Dilgo Khyentse (*din*-go *chyent*-sey) Rinpoche for fourteen years. Khyentse Rinpoche was extremely accomplished, and renowned as both a scholar and a meditator. As a young man he'd meditated in a cave for twelve years and reached an extremely high state of accomplishment as a yogi. He went on to master the scholarly teachings of many lineages, and was the leader of the Tibetan Buddhist Rimey (ecumenical) Movement.

For example, Khyentse Rinpoche was the head of the Nyingma Lineage, yet he'd taught and exchanged empowerments with His Holiness the Dalai Lama XIV, head of the Gelugpa Lineage. The Nyingma Lineage is possibly the most populous of the major Tibetan lineages, and Khyentse Rinpoche remained its leader until his passing into Paranirvana in 1991, leaving behind many relics in his body.

While studying under his constant guidance, Tulku Sangak Rinpoche served Khyentse Rinpoche for the last fourteen years of Khyentse Rinpoche's life, helping to create his temple in exile and train the monks, presiding over the three-year retreat cloister, presiding over the seminary for several years, watching over the monastery when he didn't accompany Khyentse Rinpoche on his many travels, presiding over the monastery for several summer retreats, building stupas, and helping in many other ways.

A few years ago Khyentse Rinpoche's grandson, Rabjam Rinpoche, now running Khyentse Rinpoche's monasteries, asked Tulku Sangak Rinpoche to teach Dzogchen to the highest masters of the monastery, because Tulku Sangak Rinpoche knew better than anyone the system that Khyentse Rinpoche had taught. Tulku Sangak Rinpoche continues these teachings today.

Coming to America

Tulku Sangak Rinpoche first heard of America when he was eight years old. For no apparent reason he was immediately taken with it and thought of nothing else for a week. He told himself, "When I grow up, I'm going to live there."

He had countless visions of America. One was of the land that has become his main center in America, in Arlee, Montana. As we drove around one day, looking for a spot for this center, we thought it would be good to find a piece of land along the main local highway, 93. We wandered onto a sheep ranch, just off the highway, that Rinpoche seemed to respond to immediately. Later he told me he'd recognized that exact view from one of his visions at the age of eight. In the center of the land is a flat-topped butte, and there are mountains in the distance, surrounding the viewer in all directions—an unusual geological feature which Rinpoche mentioned at the time. After he had lived in Arlee for a couple of years, he had—and has now achieved—a dream to build a statue garden of huge proportions on that piece of land. He called it The Magadha Garden of One Thousand Buddhas. The central statue, the Great Mother, standing over twenty-five feet tall, is filled with extremely holy relics, and is surrounded by the thousand buddhas of this aeon, as well as a thousand stupas.

Over the millennia, the Tibetans have developed to a high art the ability to fix and radiate pure realized mind. Through sacred architecture, mantra (archetypal sound), and many other methods, they can ground that realized mind with a sort of giant tuning fork, which then sounds that note. Although we're not consciously aware of it, we have the ability to fall in tune with that note. Since everything emanates from pure mind/awareness, at our core we are pure mind as well. Because that true essence is covered over by distraction and confusion, we don't realize this true nature. Structures such as these, filled with relics such as these, "infect" us with the realization of that pure nature. We become entrained to that strong note being sounded, and naturally fall into a peaceful, happy, more awake state. We'll explore these ideas much further throughout this book. For now I'll just say that the relics are a key ingredient, as are the methods that expand the power of that ingredient.

A statue or stupa can be empowered in this way. Not only is Rinpoche aware of this phenomenon, but he has become a master at building stupas in order to help beings far into the future. After all, stupas last for hundreds, sometimes thousands, of years. With that ripple effect in mind, he has offered this pilgrimage site so that

Americans can be "infected" by Buddha Mind, simply by bringing themselves there.

Prayer Changing Water

Many of you may know of the work of Dr. Masaru Emoto. He has spent many years photographing water before and after prayer has been directed at it, or words have been pasted on the jars containing the water. He takes microscopic photographs of the frozen water crystals before and afterward. The differences are dramatic.

"Thank You"   *"You Fool"*

He has tried the same sort of experiment with music, with similar effects.

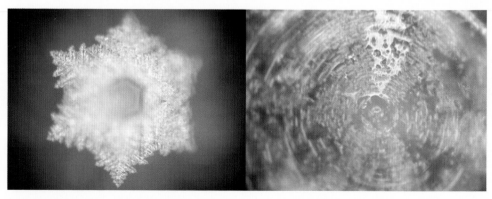

Beethoven Symphony No. 5   *Heavy Metal Music*

Some of you may also know of the work of Rupert Sheldrake, and the term he coined, *morphic resonance*, the title of his first book on the subject. His double-blind studies, which have been replicated worldwide, are accepted by many scientists.

In one experiment, he had people memorize lists of words, in a random order. The control group had a new list, and the experimental group had the list that other groups had been memorizing. The second group learned that same list faster, and subsequent groups even faster, as the experiment continued. The control groups learned at the same rate each time.

Other scientists who were working on crystal formation considered this a possible explanation for a phenomenon that had baffled them for decades. The first time they formed a new crystal pattern, it was extremely difficult to coax the substance to come together in that new formation. But as they formed that same one again and again, even in laboratories on different continents, with different scientists, it was progressively easier.

Sheldrake's theory was that these patterns are not localized—that *knowledge* is not localized. This would explain not only both of the above observations, but many other, previously unexplainable phenomena. For example, Sheldrake has since done many experiments with pets and their owners: though unable to see or hear each other, the pets somehow measurably respond to what is happening with their unseen owners. These results have been repeated again and again, with different pets and owners, in different locations.

Back to Dr. Emoto and his water crystals. His work became highly celebrated in Japan, and with his encouragement, thousands of people have conducted their own similar experiments. He even sells photographic equipment for the experiments on his website, producing more results supporting his theory that our thoughts and intentions have a measurable effect on water.

Given that it's water that he has seen these results with, and water is the pervasive medium of life on earth, the implications are huge. We ourselves are made up of more than two-thirds water, as is the food we eat.

One famous experiment was done with rice—this being Japan and all. Identical cooked rice was combined with the same kind of water and placed at the same time in two identical jars, one with "you fool" pasted on it, the other with "thank you." The rice was kept in the same room for one month. During this time several people talked to each jar, saying "you fool" to the "you fool" jar, and "thank you" to the other. After one month, the "thank you" jar had turned a soft yellow and smelled sweetly fermented. The other had turned blackish and its smell was intolerable.

"You Fool" (Left) and "Thank You" (Right)

A far more dramatic experiment was done with one of the largest lakes in Japan, Lake Biwa. In July of 1999, 350 people gathered at the lake, which had become so polluted that the native plants had been overrun by an extremely foul-smelling algae called *kokanada*, nearly covering the lake. Every year the government would get calls from a large surrounding area, complaining of the fetid smell. No doubt the wildlife whose home was in and around the lake was also affected. Though the government had spent large amounts of money in a heroic effort to discourage the algae, their efforts had had little effect. A widely known saying claimed that "if the water of Lake Biwa could be cleaned up, so could the rest of Japan's water." But no one knew how to make that happen. It seemed hopeless.

And so the crowd had gathered, armed with prayer and intention—nothing more, nothing less. After some instructions on breath control, they all repeated the Great Declaration ten times and cheered; then the prayer fest was over. The words to the Great Declaration, which helped the participants direct their thoughts and intentions, are "The eternal power of the universe has gathered itself to create a world with true and grand harmony."

Next summer, the kokanada was hardly to be found, and no one reported any foul smell. The government and scientists had no explanation. By August the phenomenon was being written up in the newspapers.

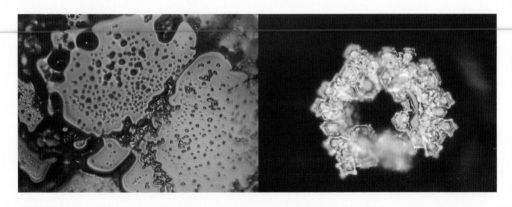

Lake Biwa Water Before Prayer   **Lake Biwa Water After Prayer**

If the Buddha was right and we manifest our bodies from mind, and there really is one big awareness, then it all makes sense. If we see all this from only the view of Newtonian physics, which today's scientists no longer hold to be entirely true, then there is no explanation.

Though Dr. Sheldrake's work is accepted by many scientists, Dr. Emoto's is not as widely embraced. One sticking point is that Dr. Emoto doesn't do double-blind studies: the people photographing the water know which word is on which jar. According to Heisenberg's Principle, the experimenter's own expectation and knowledge can affect the material being experimented on. But to my way of thinking, if that is indeed happening, wouldn't that further support Dr. Emoto's theory?

Another objection is that Dr. Emoto doesn't let us see all of his photographs. Perhaps he's picking out particular crystals to support his theory. That could be true. But now that home kits are available, and so many people are replicating his experiments and sharing their results, that concern has lessened in my mind. And if his theory were untrue, how could Lake Biwa have been transformed so dramatically and measurably? Still, I think it would be better if he shared *all* of his photographs with scientists and others, so that we could get a more complete understanding of the phenomenon.

That said, I do find the photographs and experiments he does show us compelling. The implications are powerful, not only for cleaning up water pollution. As one mother said regarding the sunflower that experimenters had attacked with the word "fool" for all its poor, stunted life, it's deeply concerning to correlate the effect of such negativity on a flower with the way that many parents view

"*Beautiful*"   "*Ugly*"

and speak to their children. And the implications for how we treat our world and each other reach far beyond even that.

A Tibetan monk was once asked what he thought of these ideas about water, and whether Buddhism has any practices concerning this. "This is completely consonant with Buddhism," he replied. "Since our own bodies are mostly water, why not just say mantras, visualize, and so on, and affect the water that's already inside us?" He smiled in a bemused way. "This seems the most direct method."

Crystal Formed After Exposure to Buddhist Chant:
Namu myoho renge kyo
(Devotion to the Mystic Law of the Lotus Sutra)

WHY THE BUDDHA BOTHERED

From Prince to Buddha

Once, thousands of years ago, there were a king and queen of a small but prosperous land. One day the queen gave birth to a golden, glowing baby boy. The wise men of the court could all see that he was exceptional. A greatly revered master suddenly appeared at the court. He predicted that if the infant chose to be king, he would be ruler of all the known world. If he chose to lead a contemplative life, he would conceive a great world religion. Just as mysteriously, the master left.

As with many fathers, the king wanted to make sure the young prince went into the family business. As with many sons, Siddhartha had other leanings, but I'm getting ahead of myself.

To keep the young prince interested in worldly affairs, the king decided he needed to do two things. First, he needed to make sure Siddhartha never suffered, nor saw any suffering. Then he wouldn't feel moved by compassion to pursue a spiritual path. Second, he provided young Siddhartha with all the earthly pleasures one could possibly desire.

As the prince grew up, he never saw any old people, never saw anything die, and was surrounded by lavish beauty at every turn. By the time he was almost of marrying age, the king was throwing him huge parties, with multitudes of the most beautiful musicians and dancing girls.

Siddhartha was actually bored by all this. It was without meaning for him. He became restless, and began to pressure his father to let him go out and see the world. At first the king objected, but then he arranged a grand outing, taking great care to hide any suffering whatsoever, and surrounding the prince with pleasurable things. They went on this grand outing, which was more like a parade than an exploration, and Siddhartha's restlessness only grew stronger. It was not to be denied.

An exceptional youth, stellar in intellectual, artistic, and athletic pursuits, Siddhartha knew perfectly well that everything around him was being orchestrated, contrived. He wanted to see the truth.

He asked his charioteer to take him out of the palace secretly. The charioteer agreed.

Out they went, on the road to town. Before they'd gone very far they came upon an old man, leaning on a stick. Siddhartha said, "Stop the chariot! What's wrong with that man?! His voice is hoarse, his hair is thin and white, his body is all twisted, and the little bit of flesh he has hangs from his bones in the strangest way. He can't walk without leaning on a stick. The poor man! What's happened to him?"

"That man is simply old," replied the charioteer. "He's lived maybe seventy or eighty years, and his body is falling apart. It happens to all of us, over time."

"No! Isn't there *something* we can do? Look how he's suffering with every step!"

"There's no cure for old age, or the pain and suffering that come from it. Our bodies fall apart after a while."

"Oh, this is awful. Every living being experiences this? I can't stand the thought of it! I've got to go home right now!"

The charioteer immediately took Siddhartha home, and he went straight to his room. He stayed there alone for days, overcome with grief for the pain of everyone and everything—any being who is born—suffering the deterioration of old age.

> In the end what you don't surrender
> Well the world just strips away.
> — BRUCE SPRINGSTEEN

As you can imagine, the king was horrified. Since his son's birth, he'd lavished great expense and effort to keep all unpleasant sights from the palace grounds, yet his greatest fear was coming to pass. He ordered an even wider radius around the palace for banishment of all unpleasant sights.

After Siddhartha had recuperated a bit, he asked his charioteer to take him for another outing. Out they went—outside the boundary, of course. This time, they soon came upon someone who was very sick. He was laid out on a pallet by the road. He had boils all over his body, a high fever, and was groaning and writhing in pain.

"Now, what's wrong with *this* person?" Siddhartha asked, again distraught at the intolerable suffering before him.

"That person is sick. At some time in life, every being gets sick." The prince went to help the man. "No, no!" cried the charioteer. "If you try to help him you won't be able to, but you'll catch the disease yourself! You must get back in the chariot!"

At this the prince felt unbearable grief and helplessness. "Please take me back."

Once again he stayed alone in his room for days, contemplating the implications of what he'd just seen. Once again, the helpless king widened the boundary around the palace.

Soon the prince asked for yet another outing. The charioteer complied once again. This time they came upon a man who was dying. "Stop the chariot!" the prince exclaimed. He then watched in horror as the man stared about in terror, struggling weakly, limbs trembling aimlessly, feebly. Then he stopped moving. His breathing lengthened until the last breath came out. Then his body shuddered and was still.

"What was *that*?!" the prince cried.

"That was death. That person died. Every sentient being that is born has to go through that. There's nothing anyone can do. You and I will die too, one day. I'm sorry, Your Highness."

Once again the prince returned home, inconsolable. He thought and thought about the vast suffering that was in the world. He contemplated how that suffering could be relieved; he knew that he had absolutely no answer.

He knew that he wanted to always be happy and never suffer. He knew that *everyone* wants to be happy and free from suffering—not just for a moment but always—just as he did. He also now knew that our best efforts were not enough to make that happen.

In fact, quite often, the more fervently we try to push away suffering and pursue happiness, the more suffering we call upon ourselves. He himself had gone on these outings because he was suffering, feeling like a bird in a golden cage. Yet with each foray into the outer world, he felt far worse. His father had thrown one huge party after another, and Prince Siddhartha had watched the guests drinking and overeating, in pursuit of happiness—their reward an upset stomach, at best.

How can we actually achieve lasting happiness? He resolved that he absolutely *must* find the answer, at all costs. He knew that to find that answer, he needed to see reality and the nature of the mind *as it truly is*. But how could he do that?

He went out one more time. This time Siddhartha saw a thin man in thin rags, with a walking stick and a small bowl. The most striking thing to the prince was that this man was happy—in fact, he was the happiest person Siddhartha had ever seen! He looked like a beggar, which the prince had seen on his recent outings, but instead of abject misery, this fellow radiated joy. "Who's that?" he asked the charioteer. "That's a mendicant, a spiritual seeker." Now Siddhartha knew what to do.

He resolved that, for the sake of all suffering beings, he had to answer this great question once and for all: How can we be completely free from suffering, and experience ultimate joy without end? He knew that the answer did not lie within the palace walls, but with spiritual masters. One night, just before dawn, he escaped.

He wandered for many years, eating only what people gave him in his begging bowl, studying from some of the greatest masters of the day. At last he had surpassed all of them. Yet he still had not quite come to see naked reality, without even the slightest veil of his own interpretations. He hadn't found the key to ultimate, lasting happiness.

So he spent many more years starving himself and following other ascetic practices, but came to the end of that, too. He concluded that abusing his body was not an effective path to enlightenment. At last, still short of his goal, he sat down under a bodhi tree with huge, heart-shaped leaves, vowing to meditate on that spot without rest, until he reached complete enlightenment.

He stayed awake all day and all night, holding his consciousness in a steady, pure state. Many unbelievably compelling temptations and distractions appeared, but he held firm. At last, with the waters of his mind completely calm for the entire night, he attained total enlightenment. He had passed the point of no return to the confused perception of the world that we all have. He had fully awakened from the confused dreamlike state that we mistake for true reality and that is actually the source of our suffering. He was now in a state of perpetual bliss, from which he never had to depart. He had now realized the secret of eternal happiness. He had attained it.

Shortly after his enlightenment, he was walking down the road. Struck by his brilliantly radiant presence and visible aura, a passerby stopped and asked him, "Are you a deity?"

"No."

"Are you a sorcerer, then?"

"No."

"An ordinary man?"

"No."

"Well, then, what are you?"

"I am awake."

In Sanskrit, the word for "awakened one" is *Buddha.*

At that time he already had a few students. When they saw that he had gained total enlightenment, and achieved eternal happiness, they said, "Please teach us, so we can be fully enlightened too!"

"I would love to, if only I could portray it in words. True reality is beyond concepts. Anything we can think of, or put into words, is not true reality. In that case, how can I teach it, or even talk about it?"

"But you can't just *leave* us here to suffer and die, again and again! Please do *something* to help us!"

And so began the famous teachings of the Buddha, which we know today as the Dharma. In giving us the Dharma (literally, "Truth" in Sanskrit), he gave us the methods by which we all can come to experience what he had experienced, the reality he now always abided in.

But he didn't ask them to practice these methods just because he said to; he felt that blind faith wasn't worth much. He asked them to try the methods for themselves, to see if they worked for *them*. The faith of our own experience is unshakable. We can't *un-know* something, once we've come to know it for ourselves.

The Buddha lived, wrote, and taught these methods for many, many more years, establishing the first Buddhist *Sangha*, or spiritual community, the foundation for Buddhism as we know it today.

The three pillars common to all traditions within the Buddhist path are the Buddha, the Dharma, and the Sangha. Together they're called the Three Jewels. You've just now learned these words; later I'll explain why these three things are so very essential to our reaching the goal of this path. For now, let's go back to the Buddha.

Recognizing that we all have different styles of learning and different proclivities, he created a vast body of works, with several different basic courses of training, to meet our various needs. All of his many thousands of sutras and tantras have been saved and translated into all of the world's languages. All of the major methods for training the mind have been practiced, mastered, and carefully handed down, mouth-to-ear, mind-to-mind, from master to student, until the present day.

We can see, then, why the Buddha bothered to reach enlightenment. He had hoped from the outset of his quest that he could offer people a path other than running after happiness, only to bring more suffering on themselves in the process. He set out to help us to save ourselves from the painful cycle of birth, leading to old age, sickness, and death. Many have attained full enlightenment using his methods.

Even in recent times there have been eyewitness accounts of people attaining "rainbow body," leaving behind nothing but their hair and nails. Thousands of others showed signs of attaining enlightenment at the time of death, leaving mantra syllables on their bones and relics inside their bodies, for example.

So the Buddha Shakyamuni, as he is called by Tibetans, was spurred on by the highest motivation, known as the Two Purposes: enlightenment for self and enlightenment for others. He gained complete enlightenment in order to help all of the rest of us to be eternally happy and free of suffering, and to be more joyfully and compassionately alive as we make the journey toward enlightenment.

RECOMMENDED READING

For a lovely introduction to the idea that happiness is something we can actually learn, just like playing the piano, I highly recommend the book *Happiness*, by Matthieu Ricard. It's short, to the point, and very readable, with lots of great stories and examples. Ricard also cites some fascinating recent studies on the effect of Buddhist practice on brain function. For example, wouldn't it be nice to be able to focus your mind on one thing and have it stay there? It's possible to train in that. But the trainings go far beyond that one capacity. His book tantalizes us with some of the results.

For example, Chapter 16 quotes scientific studies on the brain that show "off the charts" positive brain functions in longtime meditators. Even fairly new meditators begin to show measurable results. If you're tempted to read Chapter 16 first, it's all right with me. The book you have in your hands gives some of the same beginning, traditional Tibetan mind-training methods that Ricard speaks of in his book and practices himself.

Ricard is a highly accomplished monk who trained and worked alongside Tulku Sangak Rinpoche, under His Holiness Dilgo Khyentse Rinpoche. Before he was a monk, he was a physicist. Tulku Sangak Rinpoche holds Ricard in the highest esteem.

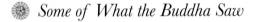 *Some of What the Buddha Saw*

The Four Noble Truths

The Truth of Suffering

The Truth of the Origin of Suffering

The Truth of the End of Suffering

The Truth of the Path

THE FOUR NOBLE TRUTHS

As you remember, when the Buddha first saw reality as it truly is, he was reluctant to try to put it all into words, a task he deemed impossible. Still, when his students begged him not just to leave them to wander hopelessly in Samsara, he began to teach.

From then until the end of his life, he taught the methods and understandings that, if his students held to them and followed them, could guide them to their own experience of true reality— enlightenment. Then no words would be necessary. They would not need to take anything on blind faith because they would know for themselves, from their own experience.

As you've noticed, I've attempted to describe some key aspects of reality that the Buddha talked about, but of course the truth is much different from the words you've been reading. Not only is my explanation flawed because it's expressed in words, but more to the point, I'm only a sentient being lost in Samsara myself, not a buddha. Thankfully, as we all know, the Buddha did go on to teach the methods for seeing reality for ourselves, in all its truth and fullness. The first teaching he gave was the Four Noble Truths, which I'll just briefly introduce you to here. I strongly suggest you read about them in depth—for example, in *The Words of My Perfect Teacher* by Patrul Rinpoche or in the book and video *The Four Noble Truths* by His Holiness the Dalai Lama.

The Four Noble Truths are the Truth of Suffering, the Truth of the Origin of Suffering, the Truth of the End of Suffering, and the Truth of the Path.

THE TRUTH OF SUFFERING

The first is the Truth of Suffering. You'd think after all this time we've spent suffering, we'd understand it very well. Maybe not. We might be able to free ourselves from it permanently if we understand the true nature of suffering, as the Buddha did.

For example, there's the "Suffering of Suffering," as in the straight-up pain of a toothache. Then it often compounds: we spend an afternoon in a dentist's chair. That's followed by the bill. Besides that, it's 40°F and pouring rain, and we have to work outside with our tooth still tender.

Of course even in Samsara there are happy times. But sadly, they come to an end. So there's the "Suffering of Change," which follows all happy moments. The chocolate I'm eating will be all gone in a few minutes, alas. Maybe something else in that last delicious meal gave us food poisoning and we suffer terribly, a short time later. Or we simply go to a great party that, of course, comes to an end.

I knew a couple who enjoyed the "holy grail" for most Westerners: a happy marriage. They worked and played together all the time. After ten years together she died of cancer. And even if she hadn't gotten cancer, eventually one of them would have died, then the other.

The third category is the "Suffering of Conditioning" (the condition of Samsara). Let's look at this one a bit more, since it's not as obvious as the first two, though it pervades our existence. As I've explained, there is a problem with the whole movie we call *existence*, inherent in the very setup. Everything in that movie is a conglomeration, and every conglomeration is unstable because it's in constant flux and eventually comes apart altogether. Even the earth and the sun will eventually fall apart. Science hasn't come up with an antidote to that one yet.

The Buddha saw that, just as with a movie, existence is constantly flashing forth, frame by frame, and disappearing into emptiness in between. Every frame of the movie emerges from darkness, slightly different from the previous one, but we don't perceive that difference. We also don't perceive the emptiness between the flashing images. We put the flashing images into a smooth line, experiencing them as an unbroken flow. As with a movie, we get

completely wrapped up in the drama. We laugh and cry, forgetting that we're sitting in a theater or watching our TV. So it is with Samsara. The scary thing is that we're the lousy *writers and producers* of this movie, *and we don't even know it!* We don't know it's a movie, much less our *own* production.

Coming from a Jewish background, when I found myself in painful circumstances, I'd sometimes give God the finger. Literally. Quite a contrast to many of the Tibetans' enlightened approach to their experience of the Chinese occupation. It wasn't until much later that I realized that I was the author and producer of my movie. That puts quite a different perspective on things.

As little specks of reality, we're actually quite hard to please. We're cold, so we go out and sit in the sun. Then we sweat, get uncomfortable with the heat, mutter at the sun, and go back inside. We cry tears of joy at weddings, and a short time later the newlyweds are often in a pitched battle, crying tears of frustration and anger.

The very nature of waves is that they go up and down. So if we identify ourselves as waves, we're going to suffer when we get to the part where "our" wave goes down. We'll suffer as our bodies fall apart. We'll suffer when the people and things we love fall apart, but they're waves, appearances, too.

All Samsaric situations are suffused with karma and confusion, like poison concealed in healthy-looking food. So this last form of suffering speaks of the truth of suffering inherent in all things in our existence, even if we don't see the suffering coming. This last form of suffering tends to sneak up on us.

Student: *Is karma always negative?*

LT: There are both negative and positive traces we can put on our mindstream. The Tibetans generally use different words for each: karma for the negative, and merit for the positive. These work a lot like debit and credit, on a great karmic ledger. If there is a negative balance, we're either experiencing unhappy times, or we soon will be. When we finish a painful experience, that would indicate that we've paid that "karmic debt." On the other side, if we've been having a wonderful time and that comes to an end, we've just spent down some merit balance until it's exhausted. The workings of karma constitute a vast subject, and the Tibetans have looked into it quite deeply. I can only hope to introduce you and give you a general feeling for karma and merit in this book. I will say a bit more as we go along, though.

THE TRUTH OF THE ORIGIN OF SUFFERING

This can be boiled down to the Three Poisons, which are the root causes of all the suffering of Samsara , the three categories of neurotic emotions: ignorance/delusion, desire/clinging, and anger/aversion. And these three, in turn, can be boiled down into one Mother of All Root Causes: identifying as "I" instead of the whole ocean. One wave would be only one very small part of the vastness of the ocean. Yet our own "wave" fills our entire mental world—our movie is only about us. Actually, the real movie is about the entire ocean … which includes our own tiny wave. Quite a different viewpoint.

The word in Latin for "I" is *ego*. Maybe you've read or heard about "letting go of ego," or ego being the whole problem. It's not the ego, or anything else in existence, that's the problem. It's what we DO about it, first and

> *The secret is*
> *identifying with the whole ocean,*
> *instead of just one wave.*

foremost in our minds, that's the problem. It's the identifying as only being "I," and clinging to that "reality," that keeps us going around on the Wheel of Samsara.

The secret is identifying with the whole ocean, instead of just one wave.

THE TRUTH OF THE END OF SUFFERING

Here the Buddha was assuring us that we could indeed free ourselves from this Wheel of Samsara. Once the Buddha saw reality as it truly is and reached the point of no return (to Samsara), he was no longer tempted to follow after thoughts of grasping, aggression, and so on. He no longer had a reason to. The domino effect was reversed and stopped at its source.

We now know that, since we're made of Buddha Nature, we too can reach the end of all suffering, permanently. We can finally end our wandering and go back Home. For good.

THE TRUTH OF THE PATH

The Buddha laid out the actual methods for us to achieve this goal. He taught thousands and thousands of verses, including the sutras and tantras. In their various ways they outlined and explained the knowledge and methods that lead to enlightenment. The whole of his teachings is what is meant by the word *Dharma*, the "path" for the followers of the Buddha. In Sanskrit, the

word *Dharma* means "truth." It also means "phenomena." The homonym for the Tibetan word for Dharma—*chö*—means "to adjust" or "to correct." Anam Thubten Rinpoche points out that *chö* also means "to change, transform, from within." When we put all of these dimensions of meaning together, a richness emerges that in itself helps us on our way.

To give us more clarity about how to tread this path of liberation from Samsara, the Buddha laid out in his first teachings eight aspects, like eight strands woven together to make a very strong rope. He called them the Eightfold Noble Path: Right View, Right Thought, Right Speech, Right Conduct, Right Livelihood, Right Effort, Right Mindfulness, and Right Concentration. This is foundational to all branches of Buddhism, so there is a great deal

written about this, but here I'm just mentioning it in the context of the Four Noble Truths.

If you'd like to explore this more, I highly recommend the piece "The Eightfold Noble Path" that a Western monk, Bhikkhu

Bodhi, has written; he has written about the Eightfold Noble Path in a short online piece and as a more detailed book.

The Eightfold Noble Path is so foundational that I highly recommend that you read and contemplate it further. In general, again, these are all aspects of conduct that help us to tread the path of liberation from Samsara, from suffering, to perfect happiness that never ends. This, then, is the fourth Noble Truth—the Truth of the Path.

We can boil these Four Noble Truths down into one sentence: *once we understand the truth of suffering and the truth of its origins, we're ready to hear about the truth of the end of such sufferings and to tread the true path.*

Perhaps now it's clear why the Buddha started all his teachings with the Four Noble Truths.

 *The Two Truths*

Absolute Truth
<hr>
Relative Truth
<hr>

These Two Truths are not included in the Four Noble Truths; they are more like two different *realities* that the Buddha is referring to. Perhaps you've been wondering how to resolve the Absolute Truth that we've been talking about with your very real experience of actions and consequences, self and other, the more pedestrian everyday reality that somehow still seems awfully true. Good question! Actually, it's a huge question, one we won't fully succeed in resolving until we're fully certified buddhas.

What the Buddha had to say about this makes a lot of sense. He spoke of the *Two* Truths and warned that allegiance to only one will leave you in confusion. The first truth, known as Absolute (or Genuine or Ultimate) Truth, is utterly simple and consistent. It's what everything else boils down to, well, ultimately: one absolute truth.

Relative Truth is quite another matter. First, it refers to all appearance—anything other than the vast emptiness/awareness we've talked about. Second, it refers to our warped vision of reality, which sees appearances *relative to* our own corner of the Samsaric dream, the channel we're fixated on. On the level of Relative Truth, water is not consistently one thing. To us, it's something to drink. To a fish, it's home and it's something to breathe; if we made our home in the lake where a fish lives, we'd die in a few minutes. To beings on other planes that we can't tune into, it is yet something else. For example, to a being of a hot hell realm, a river is molten, flaming, and lava-like. To a member of a god realm, it's *amrita*, wisdom nectar, more delightful than anything you or I can even conceive of. Relative Truth is conditioned by the eye of the beholder.

Here's another aspect of Relative Truth: if you're caught in Samsara, then the laws of karma are going to apply to you—just as the laws of gravity, or the pain when somebody twists your nose, are all very real.

This is why we need to take both truths into account. If we ignore the laws of karma before we're enlightened and therefore free of them, we're making a grave mistake. And if we don't recognize that an Absolute Truth underlies our daily reality, we're going to remain stuck.

I know of a highly accomplished American Zen practitioner who had spent so much time focusing on Absolute Truth that he felt he could ignore the consequences of his actions because they weren't "real." This caused pain for many in his wake, and planted karmic seeds for him.

I hasten to add that there are mistakes made by practitioners of Vajrayana (Tibetan Buddhism), too. I mention some at the end of this section, so I won't go into them here. Since all branches of all religions are peopled by sentient beings, we will find misinterpretations within all of them. As a friend of mine said when somebody once caught her getting angry, "I'm a Buddhist, not a buddha!"

The Two Truths make up two sides of *one* coin—one whole picture of reality. The practices of Vajrayana are designed, from beginning to end, to help us hold both of those in a vast, ever more clear-eyed view.

Tibetan Use of Imagery—Bringing It All onto the Path

The Tibetans understand well how we can create real experiences for ourselves through imagery. These methods have been tested and refined for thousands of years, on millions of people. Our Western methods of psychology are brand new compared with that!

Tibetans speak of the 100 Peaceful and Wrathful deities, and there are finely honed practices associated with them. Some of the deities are breathtakingly beautiful and peaceful, others fierce and fearsome. Each has its own particular quality and capacities. Each image evokes a particular archetype, a principle of reality or aspect of enlightened mind.

As we focus on a particular archetypal deity, we also use archetypal sound, called *mantra*. Again, the ancient science of evoking these wisdom presences through sound formulas is highly refined and proven effective.

In fact, through mantra, dance, prostrations, using the mala (rosary) as we count our mantras, burning incense, and celebrating sacred feasts, we engage all our senses in the process of awakening, including the thinking consciousness that Buddhists recognize as a sixth sense. Rather than blocking out the world and our experience of it, the Tibetan form of Buddhism, Vajrayana, brings everything right onto the path of awakening. It even served Rinpoche to transform his prison experience into one of a pureland (a Buddhist form of heavenly realm sometimes called a *Buddhafield*).

As long as we're so caught up in our sensory experience and thinking minds, why not *use* it all by pointing our senses in the direction we'd like to go—enlightenment? As I'd asked myself so many years ago, do we have something better to do?

WHAT'S SAMSARA, AND HOW DID WE GET HERE, ANYWAY?

I am bound
Upon a wheel of fire, that mine own tears
Do scald like molten lead.
KING LEAR, ACT IV

It seems absolutely basic to ask this question before we go any further. Sure, it's interesting to look at aspects of reality, but for us a more immediate question is how do we, as we know ourselves, fit into that reality? To answer that, we need to explore the meaning and origins of Samsara.

If reality is this lovely, pure stuff that we've been talking about, what's the reality we're actually faced with every day? How does *that* fit in? How did we get to all the suffering of birth, old age, sickness, and death that the Buddha was so horrified by, and why is it so hard to stop?

First I'll take us back to that one great ocean of emptiness/ awareness/compassion/wisdom, out of which all manifestation is constantly flashing forth—the ocean and its waves. So far it's all quite lovely—no problem.

But what if one wave gets a little confused and thinks it's separate from that ocean? What if it says, "I'm me, and everyone— everything else—is, well, everything and everyone else"? This sets in motion the chain reaction/domino effect we referred to earlier.

🌀 The Slippery Slope

It goes like this: If I'm just this one little wave on this vast ocean, all of a sudden I have LOTS of needs! When I was the whole ocean I didn't need anything, but now I need to protect myself from other waves that might crash into me. And I need enough water to stay together (for us humans that's food, clothing, shelter, car, job, etc.—oh, heck, and a lover and a vacation in Hawaii, too!).

Then too, as the whole ocean—one awareness—I knew everything about the whole ocean. As one little wave who's now cut myself off from the rest of the ocean, I know practically nothing.

The worst part is that all waves go up and down. I see that around me. And that means that eventually I, this little wave, will not only have my "ups and downs," but eventually I will disappear.

Because of this one confused perception—identifying as this

one wave—*everything* is different. I'm constantly either reaching for the things I personally crave or pushing away the things I personally fear and need to keep away.

If you take the time to watch your thoughts and actions really closely, I think you'll notice that those two impulses—grasping at and pushing away, two of the Three Poisons we talked about earlier—are the driving forces behind them *all*.

The internal conversations of your mind, if you boil them down, are really about those two constant efforts. The lens through which we see everything and everyone becomes colored with the ongoing questions, "Is this good for me? Is this bad for me? How do I keep this away? How do I get that?" And of course, it's also colored by the severely limited awareness that is ignorance/delusion, the third of the Three Poisons.

Those basic pervasive feelings, the Three Poisons (desire/clinging, anger/aversion, and ignorance/delusion) drive each other. Here's how it works: delusion, the misperception of reality, is *marigpa*, or *timuk*—lack of awareness, or dimness. As soon as we perceive reality in that unaware, confused way (I'm this separate wave on the ocean), we're suddenly very small and needy. That brings us to desire/clinging: in all the universe, we cling to this one form, our body. We grasp at all the things that this one form wants and thinks it needs.

When I was younger, snuggling with the man I was with felt really good, ecstatic, in fact. I could have just enjoyed the pleasure of that moment, then let go and enjoyed the next moment. But this isn't what I did. I clung as hard as I could to that moment, wanting it to go on as long as possible—longer than possible, actually—creating difficulties for the person I was with, as well as for myself. Then I would be miserable. The person understandably tended to want to snuggle less, and then I was more miserable. This was a very quick cycle of sowing and reaping misery while wanting and grasping for happiness: action (karma) and result.

This tendency toward clinging and longing has poisoned more than one relationship. We of course all have a tendency to cling to pleasurable moments. We long for them, think about how we can get them to be longer and more frequent, and can be miserable when they pass. Enjoying a pleasurable moment in the moment doesn't create a problem, but the clinging leads to a whole drama filled with suffering.

The Tibetans often do the practice of creating a colorful, elaborate, beautiful sand mandala. The artists work in such fine detail that some lines of color are as fine as one grain of sand. They sit for long hours, often with masks over their faces, using tiny tubes to place the colored sand precisely. Such a sand mandala can take several artists several days or even weeks to create. Then at the end of the related ceremony, the entire mandala is thrown into a heap and tossed into a river.

I sat next to my father in the last month of his life, and was present just as he left his body. He didn't want to go. Of course I was going to miss him, but because of his long decline, I had already been missing him. What I felt most painfully was that I couldn't help him to let go. The day after I came home from the funeral I wrote this poem.

Even This Dream

Without food or drink for 10 days, now,
His entire occupation, winnowed down
    to breathing.
He puts his whole effort into this breath.
Then this one.
Staving off the inevitable, for
    one more breath.

The nurse comes in to take his vitals.
Yet another old man to check.
Saying, "He's comfortable."

This is *comfortable?*

He can't speak. She can't know,
Inside, the deep, far-reaching, kind hearted mind.

For minutes, hours,
Days, weeks,
I watch you by stages losing
The joy of chocolate
The joy of your wit
    making us laugh.

Long gone, the joy of travel
The joy of your work of
    helping others.

Tying your own shoes
Walking
Talking
Moving
Scratching where you itch.

It's all come down to breathing
With all your might.

Please, Dad, please
Let go.
Trade in this old body.

Let go into the loving infinite.
Home.
If only you knew,
That ending dreams
Means waking up.

If not, then starting another.

What keeps you here? Fear?
Of disappearing?
Of regrets weighing you?
Some combination of both.

This form that allows you
Entry into this dream,
Slowly, slowly, fallen apart.
A beautiful, beautiful dream.
You made it so.
I shared so much of it with you,
So gladly.

We don't want this dream to end.
But all dreams do.

Alas, alas,
Even this one too.

In the case of the mandala, we see that we're meant to enjoy and appreciate the exquisite beauty of this symbolic work of art. Yet we're not to cling.

This Poison/Passion very naturally leads to the remaining one: aversion/aggression (*shey-dang* in Tibetan), pushing away what we don't want, or pushing others out of the way of the things that we do want.

Here's an example of this toxic cycle at work:

Years ago, I was horrified when my darling, sweet little daughter wanted a block a little boy was playing with. There was desire: she wanted the block. Of course he didn't want to relinquish it to her (his desire/clinging), so of course she yanked his hair. Not surprisingly, he screamed. It naturally followed from there that she got a time-out. So the whole drama began (1) with her "looking out for number one," (2) grasping for the block so she could have it herself, (3) her act of aggression, which led (4) to her own misery. This is the slippery slope in action: delusion, clinging, aggression, karmic action, resultant suffering. And besides, she never did get to play with that block.

We've all (for the most part) developed more subtle methods of grasping and repelling, but those driving emotions are still there, still leading to words and actions that over and over again cause dramas, and misery, for ourselves and others. We feel helplessly catapulted from one unhappy episode to another, unable to stop the cycle. The word for "Samsara" in Tibetan is *Korwa*, meaning "going around and around."

In case you were wondering, the Buddha was well aware that we don't have just three emotions. He spoke of 84,000 emotions, the full range, with fine degrees of subtlety. He grouped them into these three basic categories just so we could begin to get some clarity as to the workings of our own minds.

◈ *A Bit More About Karma*

As in the example of my charming daughter (she's much more socially acceptable now, and has her own daughter to occasionally embarrass her), we know that thoughts, and the emotions that drive them, lead to action. (The word for "action" in Sanskrit is *karma*.) Just as in physics, for every action there's a reaction—or, as it's commonly expressed in the Dharma, for every action there's a result.

If the ocean of reality is really one great mind, then whatever one part of that mind says or does of course comes back to it. We *think* we're doing the action to somebody else, but that thought, word, or deed actually makes a trace on our own mindstream that we'll carry with us. We can't perceive those marks on our own mindstream; we experience them a little like when we smack a ball in a handball court and the ball eventually bounces its way back to us … usually from a different direction. We accept the physical laws of cause and effect, action and consequence. Yet we seem to find it baffling, and even unjust, when the same cause-effect principles apply predictably and inevitably to our actions toward other beings.

You see why they call them the Three Poisons. We poison ourselves with the misery of those feelings; then we commit actions that leave karmic traces on our own souls, leading to far more misery,

and keeping us going around and around. The other Tibetan name for these feelings that drive us is *nyön-mong*. In other English books on Tibetan Buddhism, you'll see that very important term translated as "afflictive emotions" (a term I often use) and "conflicting emotions," or even "neurotic emotions." Sometimes the word *passions* is used. The other term the Tibetans use, *Duk Sum*, translates directly as the Three Poisons.

From recent science, we know negative emotions can lead to health problems. From our own experience we know how a bad feeling can poison our day, our interactions, and our relationships. From the point of view of karma, they poison us in an even deeper way. In this book I'll often use the term *Poisons*. In the next section you'll see more deeply why.

How We Stay Stuck

This law of cause and effect begins to explain why some people are born into comfortable circumstances and others into really awful ones ... ONLY if I also put reincarnation into the picture. After

all, how could a baby have caused a malformed leg or an abusive parent before they were born? Although we can all relate to the idea of causes being followed by results, the result doesn't always come immediately … or even within the same lifetime. That ball on a handball court could bounce a few times before arriving back at us. In our naïveté we think that once the ball leaves our hand, it goes away. But there isn't another handball court. There's only THE handball court.

To give you a quick definition of reincarnation, I'll stick with the metaphor of the waves on the ocean. When we watch a wave go up and then down, the actual water molecules in the wave when it comes up again are not the same. The wave isn't the same shape, either. Yet there's *some* kind of momentum behind it that causes us to say that it's still the same wave. That thread of consciousness behind the various lifetimes, the consciousness that leaves the body at death, and many of us say continues on, I call the *mindstream*. This is as clear and direct a translation of the Tibetan term as I can imagine.

I once asked my Root Lama, Tulku Sangak Rinpoche, how karma could follow us after death. If we, like a wave, sink back into the ocean of the emptiness/awareness after this life, how can we reemerge into the next life with the karma from this life? He gave me a visual. He picked up a piece of paper and rolled it into a tube. Then he laid it flat again. The ends curled up. He then flattened it for a moment. It popped back up. To that demonstrative metaphor I've added the idea of a crease. Again, after flattening the paper we still see the crease, along with any curls.

That little demonstration showed me how our thoughts, words, and deeds create traces on our own mindstreams, and our habits of mind shape them, so that even after our respite in the ocean of one awareness, we reemerge with a similar shape of mind, with karmic traces (creases) still there. Each of us usually has a favorite, among the Three Poisons, that shapes both the mind and body we create.

In almost every case, those shapes and creases don't disappear until we live out the results of the actions that formed them. The Bible says, "Ye shall reap what ye sow." On the other side of the world, the Tibetans also use the metaphor of planting seeds and harvesting fruits. We don't get an apple when we plant a thistle. In our mistaken efforts to be self-serving, we plant thistles all the time, expecting apples. We resent that we end up with thistles.

When I first spent some time with Rinpoche, I heard many stories of the horrors of his life after the occupation of Tibet. He was in prison for ten years, couldn't contact his family, lived under horrible conditions, did hard labor, and was tortured, scorned, and beaten. As a psychotherapist, I naturally looked for signs of post-traumatic stress disorder (PTSD). Try as I might, I couldn't see any. Much later, Rinpoche told me that most Tibetans didn't have PTSD after such traumatic experiences. At one point, a group of psychotherapists volunteered to come to Dharamsala to greet Tibetans as they fled the turmoil in their country and escaped over the Himalayas. They expected to do some trauma work, but they, too, found almost no signs—despite horrors often worse than what Rinpoche experienced.

His Holiness the Dalai Lama and his people theorized that because the concepts of reincarnation and karma are so much a part of Tibetans, they simply saw the suffering as the ripening of some actions they'd committed in another life, since "beginningless time." This allowed them to make some sense of things, retain their self-esteem as *this* person in *this life*, and also to feel compassion for their captors, who, after all, were sowing seeds for horrible suffering for themselves in the future. Besides, the Tibetans couldn't say they were any better, since they'd obviously done something like that in another life, themselves.

This wasn't just pleasant, Sunday school theorizing; this was a powerful worldview that met the painful daily reality they were living. They mostly emerged from terrible suffering as intact, compassionate people. I think of the contrast between that and some Jews who speak of not forgiving God for the Holocaust (as though some Heavenly Father ordered it) and various Judeo-Christians who have PTSD decades after a trauma, get cancer, lose a loved one, and smolder with resentment, saying, "Why me?"

No matter where we are, or in what circumstances, we all have our ways of misguidedly pursuing happiness, all the while sowing seeds of misery. The key is that, since we identify with this tiny apparition we call "me," we pursue happiness for *ourselves*.

Have you ever noticed that the people who help others seem to be the happiest? People serving mainly their own desires don't seem to be as happy, no matter how furiously they pursue their own ends. We can only speculate, but the Dalai Lama sure *seems* to be happy all the time. Everyone gets infected by his joyful presence. This despite the fact that he has lost his country, and the Tibetan religion and culture are dying out before his eyes. On the other hand, when Hitler was at his height, he was famous for his fits of temper. I doubt he was actually very happy.

One Tibetan monk said that, once he could see the suffering on the face of his torturer, he was able to have compassion for him.

If we saw ourselves as the whole ocean, we'd already be happy and wouldn't need to be so busy pursuing anything. And of course, we'd think only in terms of happiness *for all*. In that case, why would we ever do something that would harm another? Would we even think in terms of "other"? When would we ever act without the motivation to benefit all?

So this is essentially how we stay stuck in Samsara, also called the *Wheel of Samsara*: because as we chase after happiness, we keep sowing seeds of misery. Through ignorance/delusion (the first Poison), we see things through our twisted karmic lens. Then, in this deluded state, we're driven by desire (the second Poison), as well as aversion/aggression (the third one). We follow our thoughts to their confused conclusions, then act in misguided ways that sow more karmic seeds.

This is how we stay stuck in Samsara.

Then we reap those, try to relieve the misery in the wrong way, do all that habitually, and around and around we go.

The Buddha had been on that wheel, but finally saw through the dream—gave it up altogether—and reached the point of no return, freeing him to rest in an indescribably joyful state permanently. Lucky for us—incalculably lucky—he didn't just let go and turn into rainbow light as he melted into the great ocean of oneness. Most who have attained enlightenment do that. But the Buddha carried into his last life the powerful momentum of lifetimes of compassionate intent. Even after reaching full Buddhahood, he stayed in that body and taught us the way out.

Student: *If we'd be so much happier giving up identifying with ego, and we're so miserable with it, why don't we all just give it up? What's the big deal?*

LT: The short answer: go for it! The long answer: when great masters have become enlightened, they've reported that it was a very simple moment, like letting a heavy coat drop off of you when it gets warm. The problem for the rest of us is that we're so entrenched in the reality of being this one little apparition—since beginningless time—that the idea of dropping it feels like obliteration. Since we can't really feel the whole ocean of compassionate awareness, it seems to us like we'll *vanish altogether*, and be no more. This is why we cling so desperately to our small, separate self, even in times of extreme misery. No matter how many times we read or hear that we're better off identifying with the whole ocean, and believe it with our conscious, rational mind, too much of our mindstream—our habitual, small mind—still clings to the self-perpetuating conviction that we're a separate, distinct self.

There is a Sanskrit term that puts its finger right on this conviction: "*satkaya-drsti. Sat* means real or true, *kaya*, body, and *drsti* is view; the term as a whole is usually translated 'personality-belief.' "[*]

When my daughter was fifteen years old, she took refuge with Rinpoche in a ceremony in Nepal. That night, as we were falling asleep, she said, "Mama, I really feel as if it wouldn't be a big deal to just drop it all—all that I think is me—and join with everything. But as soon as I actually try to *do* it, I realize I'm too scared." She was a very wise fifteen-year-old.

---

[*]   From: Sangharakshita, *What Is the Sangha: The Nature of Spiritual Community* (Birmingham, England: Windhorse Publications, 2000), p. 36.

THE GOOD NEWS

So I've given you the bad news … but *don't despair!* The Buddha had good news, too. Really good news. While many Christians talk about Original Sin, Buddhists talk about Original Purity. I didn't make this up! When Buddhists speak of Original Purity, they're talking about that great ocean in its true state, absolutely pure from the very beginning. So are all its waves. Every one of them. Even you and I. We merely have to "clean the windshield" of confused seeing, and we're restored to our true state. Now THAT'S good news!

If our true essence weren't that pure, aware emptiness, we could never reach enlightenment. If there's no gold ore in a stone, there's nothing we can do to get gold from it. Our true essence is like the gold ore in that stone. We have Buddha Nature, but to the untrained eye we look and act like an ordinary stone. We need to smelt the ore, to get rid of the nonessential elements and end up with the pure gold. In our case, we need to apply skillful methods so we can eventually, ultimately, refine the gold of our true selves. So enlightenment generally doesn't happen in an instant of epiphany. It's a process, just like discovering, smelting, and refining gold.

Interestingly, there were time-honored schools of alchemy in both the West and the East. Carl Jung revived those studies in the West, realizing that the "gold" the alchemists had been really concerned with was not metal; it was the soul, restored to its original purity. These alchemists' goal was very much like the refining to perfection of the mindstream that we've been talking about.

To put it simply, we need to remove the impurities of ego identification, to allow the pure gold of our true nature to shine forth, unimpeded.

The process of changing age-old habits of mind can't be instantaneous, though the last moment of crossing over to enlightenment is. Sure, it takes time and effort. But again, the question I asked myself when I set out on this journey was, "Do I have something *better* to do?"

Another traditional analogy I like is that of the sun and clouds. When clouds obscure the sun, it looks as if the sun has disappeared. But we know it's still there, shining just the same. It's just that our vision is obscured by the clouds. And even on a cloudy day, it isn't pitch dark—we can still find our way if we watch where we're going.

So it is with us. Even as we are right now, we have "buddha qualities"—evidence that we're really made of Buddha Nature. Whenever we go out of our way during the day to help someone—and feel a warm happy feeling when we do—we know we're not really so separate after all. When a stray puppy is hungry and lonely, our hearts are moved by compassion. When we feel moved by the suffering and death of people hit by a tsunami in Japan, and we've never met them and don't speak their language, why is that? According to Buddhism, it's because deep in our truest essential self, we're not actually separate from them. Many waves, one ocean.

Our true nature is Buddha Nature.

And you're taking the

time and effort to read this book because some essential core in you knows the truth and is seeking it. When something "rings true," what part of ourselves recognizes it?

I see all of these as hints that, despite the endless lifetimes in confusion, our true nature is Buddha Nature.

As we've learned, *buddha* means "awakened one." The Tibetan word for *buddha* is *sangye*, which can be broken into two parts: *sang*, meaning "cleansed," and *gye*, which means "fully matured"—in other words, *cleansing* away the clouds of karmically tainted perception and *fully maturing* our buddha (awakened) qualities.

✸ *The Three Kayas*

Once the Buddha was able to see with absolutely no veils, he saw that reality is one vast ocean of awareness. It actually has no solid substance, yet isn't just a blank vacuum.

It's aware.

Its natural quality is endless compassion, for there is truly no separation: what is felt by one part of reality is felt by the whole, vast awareness.

By its nature and power, it constantly manifests appearances, just as the ocean constantly manifests waves. As we're learning more and more in subatomic physics, we're seeing (as the Buddha saw 2,500 years ago) that these appearances aren't the substantial things we thought they were at all.

In the more obscure scientific circles which I frequent there is a legend circulating about a late distinguished scientist who, in his declining years, persisted in wearing enormous padded boots much too large for him. He had developed, it seems, what to his fellows was a wholly irrational fear of falling through the interstices of that largely empty molecular space which common men in their folly speak of as the world. A stroll across his living-room floor

LOREN EISELEY

had become, for him, something as dizzily horrendous as the activities of a window washer on the Empire State Building. Indeed, with equal reason he could have passed a ghostly hand through his own ribs.

The quivering network of his nerves, the awe-inspiring movement of his thought had become a vague cloud of electrons interspersed with the light-year distances that obtain between us and the farther galaxies. This was the natural world which he had helped to create, and in which, at last, he had found himself a lonely and imprisoned occupant. All around him the ignorant rushed on their way over the illusion of substantial floors, leaping, though they did not see it, from particle to particle, over a bottomless abyss. There was even a question as to the reality of the particles which bore them up. It did not, however, keep insubstantial newspapers from being sold, or insubstantial love from being made.

—FROM *THE FIRMAMENT OF TIME* BY LOREN EISELEY

Though it's one reality, we can speak of two aspects (emptiness/awareness and appearance), just as we can speak of both the ocean and its waves. The ocean and the waves are one thing, like two sides of one coin, but we need to have ways to talk about both aspects, so we give them names.

A Modern Physics Take—Holomovement

In the twentieth century, as Western science moved far beyond Newtonian physics, the highly regarded physicist and fellow of the Royal Society David Bohm (1917–1992), took us ahead by, well, a quantum leap. Early in his professional life, Bohm worked with Einstein, who had hoped to fully form his "unified field" theory before he died, a goal he never achieved. In my opinion, Dr. Bohm's later theories and related insights, indicated by his term *holomovement*, went far toward accomplishing the task. Perhaps in some ways they even moved beyond it.

Bohm's theories, in all their fascinating complexity, with all the vast and profound implications for our worldview, would be more than a book in themselves. In fact, Bohm did write several books and articles about his theories, but perhaps a much more succinct and understandable source would be Michael Talbot's *The Holographic Universe*. Because I didn't want this book to be all about Bohm's work, I'm including for you here just a tidbit, taken from Talbot's book. I strongly encourage you to get hold of *The Holographic Universe* and read more for yourself, though. Talbot spends most of his book exploring the implications in particular directions. I enjoyed reading pretty much the whole thing, but some of you may want to put the book down somewhere in Chapter 4; some of you early in Chapter 3. You'll know where you want to stop, or what you want to skip, when you get there.

On the way to his theory on implicate order and holomovement, Bohm was doing research the way we all would like to do it: he was watching TV. Here's what he saw one day, as described by Fred Pruyn in the August/September 1997 issue of *Sunrise* magazine.

David Bohm found confirmation of his mystic vision on television in the 1960s, when he saw a device made of two concentric glass cylinders, the space between them filled with colorless glycerin. The experimenter put a drop of ink in the glycerin, and then turned the outer cylinder. As a result, the droplet was drawn out into a thread, which gradually became thinner and thinner until it vanished completely; the ink had disappeared but still existed in the glycerin. When the cylinder was turned in the opposite direction, the ink reappeared from its enfolded, hidden existence. Bohm realized that there was no disorder or chaos, but, rather, a hidden order.

To us it would've just been a kind of cool thing. To Dr. Bohm it was life-changing. Bohm writes that "when the ink drop was spread out, it still had a 'hidden' (i.e., non-manifest) order that was revealed when it was reconstituted." After trying for years to explain many things that had remained steadfastly beyond his understanding, he now had a clue for an explanation. Then he got an even better clue: holograms.

Shortly after holographic photography was invented, I went to a laboratory where scientists were experimenting with it. They enthusiastically showed me a piece of holographic film with an image on it. It looked pretty much like any other flat piece of film, and all I could see were lots of concentric circles of various sizes, as in a pond just after a few pebbles are thrown in. I tried to look impressed. Then they shone a laser beam through it. Appearing in thin air in front of the film was a 3-D picture of chess pieces on a chess board. I was more impressed.

Then they showed me how, even if you cut that film in half, the *whole image* still shows through either half. You just have to lean a little to the left or right to see the whole thing, as though you were looking through a window that was smaller than the scene. Sure enough: I leaned side to side, seeing more of the image that had been hidden. Now I was every bit as excited as the scientists!

How does this work? Well, it's a long story, but I'll try to give you an idea in this small space. The pond circles I'd first seen, as they fanned out, crossed each other. These created incalculably complicated "interference" patterns, as they're called. In those patterns was far more information than on normal photographic film. These holograms

DAVID BOHM

stored the exponentially greater information needed to depict three dimensions, unfolded into the actual image only when the laser beam shone through it. Even more fascinating is that *every bit of the film contained the whole*. Hence the name.

That's why the half piece of film I'd looked through contained the whole picture. Perhaps you can see why Bohm got excited about holograms. Here I can't help but quote Talbot directly:

> One of Bohm's most startling assertions is that the tangible reality of our everyday lives is really a kind of illusion, like a holographic image. Underlying it is a deeper order of existence, a vast and more primary level of reality that gives birth to all the objects and appearances of our physical world in much the same way that a piece of holographic film gives birth to a hologram. Bohm calls this deeper level of reality the *implicate* (which means "enfolded") order, and he refers to our own level of existence as the *explicate*, or unfolded order.

This theory helps explain many phenomena previously unexplained by science. Though I won't go on about them all here, you can explore them through Talbot's work, and, of course, Bohm's.

I do want to quote Talbot's explanation of one previously unexplained phenomenon, because it more thoroughly clarifies the conundrum of "wavicles."

> It also explains how a quantum can manifest as either a particle or a wave. According to Bohm, both aspects are always enfolded in a quantum's ensemble, but the way an observer interacts with the ensemble determines which aspect unfolds and which remains hidden. As such, the role an observer plays in determining the form a quantum takes may be no more mysterious than the way a jeweler who manipulates a gem determines which of its facets become visible and which do not.

Perhaps this is how we can use scientific theory to illuminate the interaction between the ocean and its waves that Buddhism speaks of. Perhaps this helps us understand, too, how we create and project our own reality from the infinite possibilities enfolded within the one great awareness.

Bohm saw that the universe is constantly weaving between the implicate and explicate. For this ever-changing, moving phenomenon that Bohm wanted to point to, he wasn't satisfied with the limited, static term, "hologram." He invented the term "holo*movement*."

The Tibetans speak of three basic facets of reality.

The emptiness/awareness facet is called the *Dharmakaya*, or Truth Body. It's the ultimate, true basis behind the appearances we see.

The "waves," or appearance, aspect is divided into two more facets. One is the *Sambhogakaya*, or Body of Complete Abundance; the other is the *Nirmanakaya*, or Emanation Body. As we go from emptiness into form, we come first to Sambhogakaya. Perhaps this one is like Bohm's implicate order. The translator Sangye Khandro has sometimes described it as the Illusory, Blissful Being. How evocative! It's sort of like a template through which the power of that vast awareness can emanate into form. We don't have this exact concept in the West, but we do have a relatively new term that comes close.

You may have heard of the Western term *archetype*, popularized by Carl Jung, speaking of essential principles, such as the Great Mother principle, or the King, the Maiden, the Wise Man, and so on. We can't experience the archetypal level directly because we're stuck on the Nirmanakaya level of more fully manifested appearances—perhaps like Bohm's explicate order—as seen through

CARL JUNG
(Photo by Dimitri Kessel, The LIFE Picture Collection. Courtesy of Getty Images.)

our spattered windshields. Oh, if only we had a "channel changer" for the Kayas! This would be so much easier.

Given that we don't have a Kaya channel changer—*yet*, anyway—we can get only a subtle experience of an *archetype itself*, through an archetypal image. That's why we feel inspired when we look at some image of the Great Mother: for example, the image of Quan Yin or the Virgin Mary tends to evoke the felt experience of the purer Great Mother archetype. Though we don't have the channel changer, we use archetypal image, sound, and myth to "tune in to" the archetype itself. With very skillful methods and lots of practice, we can eventually learn to change channels at will.

But for most of us, it isn't just that we've lost the channel changer. To make matters worse, our vision is extremely altered, like a really warped, dirty, spattered, tinted windshield. What we see—though it seems absolutely real to us—has little resemblance to the Three Kayas seen with pure vision, as they truly are. Perhaps this problem relates to Bohm's theory that there are different facets of an "ensemble" contained within the implicate, and that an observer can tune in to one or another facet. So why do we zero in on one facet and not another?

Presumably, it has something to do with the shape of our own mind. Habitual points of view, for example. Our habits of *how* we chase after happiness and run from suffering determine what channel we'll fixate on. For many lifetimes we've had a vested interest in how things are going on around us—is it good for me or bad for me? This causes the fixation, making it impossible for us to freely change channels. Note that, since we don't have the channel changer, we're not *deciding* which channel, or facet, to tune in to; we fall into it and tend to stay stuck, believing that's just reality … until we die and are forced to leave that particular show.

If we start with the Dharmakaya level, the emptiness/awareness level, we then go through the archetypal-template level (Sambhogakaya), and then on to the more complex and fully manifest Nirmanakaya level. Remember that, just as the ocean and its waves aren't really separate, the Kayas are also just different aspects of the same thing—like the sun and its rays, or two sides (and the rim?) of one coin. The Kayas themselves—the ocean and its waves—are all perfectly pure; we just can't see them that way. Once we clean our windshield, we'll find the channel changer again, and see the Kayas in all their vast, pristine, and beautiful perfection. That's what the Buddha did.

❀ *The Five Timeless Awarenesses (Yeshes)*

How does this really work? Well, since we can't experience it all very directly, it's no wonder the Buddha couldn't fully put this reality into words that would make us *see* it. Words themselves carry thought forms warped and colored by our delusion (and different delusions and colorations for each of us), so there's a catch-22. Nevertheless, we can continue to use metaphor to point us in the right direction.

Another aspect of the vast Dharmakaya is a quality of wisdom/awareness that the Tibetans call *Yeshe*, or *Primordial Wisdom*. *Yeshe* has sometimes been translated as Wisdom, or Timeless Awareness (my personal favorite).

This Yeshe first divides into primal, archetypal principles of reality, spoken of as the *Five Yeshes*. These can appear as lights of five different colors, and many people have reported seeing them in near-death experiences, as well as in visions. Interestingly, people of various cultures and religions have spoken of them in pretty much the same way.

The play of Yeshe continues. These Five Yeshes weave together into an increasingly complex and dense tapestry until we get to the level of fully emanated Nirmanakaya, the waves part of the ocean. Compassion pervades the entire, vast ocean of play.

The moment we move our focus from the unity of the Dharmakaya to the Five Yeshes, we're no longer in the formless, unified Dharmakaya territory; we're speaking of the Sambhogakaya.

Here the Yeshe of the Dharmakaya now is like a five-faceted jewel: the Yeshe of Basic Space, Mirrorlike Yeshe, the Yeshe of Equality, Discerning Yeshe, and All-Accomplishing Yeshe.

Now that we're in the area of archetype (Sambhogakaya), the one state of Buddhahood is divided into the same five facets, the Five Dhyani Buddhas that are lords of the Five Buddha Families. Their names are Vairochana, Amitabha, Akshobhya, Ratnasambhava, and Amogasiddhi.

These Buddhas each have their own respective purelands, and their consciousness pervades the universe. They and their respective Yeshes are principles of reality—like fundamental archetypes—which Tibetan Buddhism makes easier to work with by applying archetypal images. They're each associated with qualities of being, colors, directions, and countless other things. They weave together in ever more complex forms to create all that appears.

Because they're not separate from anything, they feel the suffering of all the lost beings just as if it were their own ... for it is. Out of this ultimate kind of compassion that is ceaseless and endless, they are constantly weaving together all appearances—the waves of the ocean. To my mind, this idea of the Three Kayas goes beyond Bohm's concept of implicate and explicate order. Bohm points the way for Western minds, but the understanding of the Three Kayas is more fully developed, and *alive*.

Of course, because of our warped and spattered lenses we can't see all this as it really is. We only see our own deluded dream. Not only do things appear in a very warped way, but we can only see things on the channel that we're fixated on ... and we've lost the channel changer! Perhaps Bohm would say that, out of the complex array of possible facets of an "ensemble" that can "unfold" into matter, the observer's own habits of mind determine which facets will appear to their eye.

How could there be any hope of finding our way out of this dream?

As I said, the archetypal, or Sambhogakaya, level is generally impossible for us to perceive directly, but it is still very powerful and compelling, still very much at work, like a prevailing current beneath the waves of the ocean, affecting the formation of the waves on a vast scale.

From our confused, fixated vantage point of the Nirmanakaya level we can work through archetypal images, as with the earlier examples of the Great Mother archetype, so we can actually perceive something helpful, from within our own dream.

In all the world's great religions we find archetypal images of the Great Mother, such as The Virgin Mary, Quan Yin, and, in Tibetan Buddhism, Green Tara or Yum Chenmo. Our first archetypal *image* of the Great Mother is most often the face of our own mother; we already have a space in the deep recesses of our minds for the Great Mother archetype, and the image—our mother's face, and, later, cultural and artistic expressions—fills that space. Through an image we've made this connection with, we feel the vast power of the archetype itself.

Then we have our various dramas around that archetype, through the image. Archetypes are a stronger driving force behind our lives than we're conscious of, like an ocean current pulling and driving the waves along. Rather than be driven by archetypes in an unconscious, usually harmful way, why not use them to help us toward enlightenment? Why not use them to live more skillfully right now?

SCIENCE TIDBIT

In recent studies that catch the brain "in action," scientists have found that whether we are looking at an actual thing or just imagining it, *the brain acts the same way*. The same parts of the brain are stimulated, the nervous system responds the same, the same cascade of hormones and chemicals is released, and the heart changes rhythm, *whether something is out there or imagined*. Even the same muscles experience a slight activation when we just imagine the act of running!

We prove this to ourselves when we remember the death of someone we loved, imagine their face, and burst into tears. We feel a pain in our hearts, and sometimes we can hardly catch our breath. The person isn't actually in front of us, dying, but all parts of ourselves are affected as we bring that image to mind.

We imagine all kinds of things and live out experiences in our minds countless times, every day of our lives … and at night in our dreams. Wouldn't it be nice if we could *choose* which experiences to have? The Buddha, as well as the Tibetan masters, was fully aware of this phenomenon, and created practices that take full advantage of it.

🌸 The Five Dhyani Buddhas

As I've said, once Yeshe has divided into its five aspects, those five basic principles of reality, those Five Yeshes, have distinct qualities of awareness. To give us a way of relating to them on this level, we speak of the Five Dhyani Buddhas. We picture Yeshe (Timeless Awareness, or Wisdom) which of course is enlightened mind, as a buddha sitting there, with particular clothes, mantra sounds, and other characteristics that evoke the actual archetype. Each of the buddhas is the color of one of the five lights, and each can be found in their own Buddhafield, or pureland. The Five Yeshes are

Family	Buddha (Head)	Yeshe Quality	Afflictive Emotion
Buddha	Vairochana	Yeshe of Basic Space	delusion, laziness, stupidity
Vajra	Akshobhya	Mirrorlike Yeshe	aversion, aggression
Jewel	Ratnasambhava	Equalizing Yeshe	pride, inflation
Lotus	Amitabha	Discerning Yeshe	desire, longing, clinging
Karma	Amogasiddhi	All-Accomplishing Yeshe	competitiveness, jealously

referred to as "families." I'll list them for you, though once again, words are of course inadequate.

I think of these as five basic qualities, or flavors, of enlightened mind. They weave themselves into more and more complex forms. The chart indicates how they appear to us (in our confusion) as the five elements (the four we know of, plus space), the seasons, the bodily humors, the four directions plus center for the fifth, etc., etc. In fact, these five principles of reality weave themselves together into all the forms of the Nirmanakaya ... including our own physical bodies. Hence the name *Nirmanakaya*, or Emanation Body. Again, I see a correlation between Emanation Body and Bohm's explicate. But there is a vast difference between the dense bodies we think we and others have, and the non-solid, light bodies that we'd see without our spattered windshields in the way.

In sitting with this chart, maybe you can determine which family is your primary one. Tibetan medical doctors believe their patients to have manifested their bodies from their minds. If that's

Color	Direction	Element	Symbol
blue	center	space	wheel
white	east	water	vajra
yellow	south	earth	jewel
red	west	fire	lotus
green	north	air	crossed vajras

the case, then the habits and tendencies of our minds are also going to manifest in our bodies.

For example, a person more strongly aligned with the Vajra family will tend to have anger as their prominent emotion. This is because, to a greater or lesser extent, they're manifesting the deluded version of this Yeshe.

Our "family alignment" will manifest in all kinds of physical tendencies. The ongoing imbalances that create chronic diseases, as well as acute conditions, for example, will naturally follow from the habitual imbalances of the patient's mind. Even Western medicine has observed that "type A personalities," who have a choleric quality to them and are famously quick to anger, tend to have strokes and heart attacks much more often than other personality types. The doctor will be able to treat the patient systemically in a much more skillful way if they're aware of this principle.

✴ The Three Yanas

So how do we follow the doctor's advice? How do we follow this path? Fortunately the Buddha saw that we're all different, with different capacities and styles, so he didn't lay out just one path for everybody. He laid out the Three *Yanas*, or vehicles, which are like the boughs of a tree. There are a multitude of branches (twigs, even!) within those. The three major boughs, or vehicles, are Theravada, Mahayana, and Vajrayana.

Just so you know where you are on that tree, Tibetan Buddhism is the third vehicle, Vajrayana. Each of the vehicles is styled for the different karma, needs, capacities, and proclivities of different beings. Usually the karmic flow of a person's life will lead them to the path best suited for them. In America, with its veritable smorgasbord of spiritual entrees, not to mention side dishes, open bar, and vending machines, we need to feel our way through the tasting. If you find you respond best to one or another path, or come to recognize your teacher from a particular path, that path is probably yours.

One way of distinguishing among the Three Yanas is by looking at the distinct ways in which they each handle the Three Passions/Poisons. If you come upon poison, you could take one of three approaches to dealing with it. (1) You could avoid it altogether. (2) If you've already eaten it, you could take an antidote. (3) If you've already eaten it, you could also apply enough awareness that it's distilled to its purely positive quintessence. (This third approach might work better with emotions than, say, arsenic. In the case of physical poison I'd say, don't try this at home! Leave that to the masters.) With the emotion of anger, for example, when we remove all the drama and distill it to its quintessence, we have one of the Five Yeshes—Mirrorlike Yeshe.

Vajrayana meets us where we're at, with all our attending afflictive emotions, and leads us to our Buddha Nature. It uses the impure parts and helps us to smelt them like gold, to come to the pure essence.

Theravada, or School of the Ancient Ones, takes the first approach mentioned above—avoiding the poison. Mahayana, or Great Vehicle, follows the second approach—taking an antidote. Vajrayana, or Diamond Vehicle, is actually a subcategory of Mahayana, and it takes the third—distilling the poison to its pure essence.

We probably need to use all three approaches at various times, but each of us has a stronger natural inclination toward one or another of these vehicles. One of the many reasons I like the Vajrayana path is that it actually contains all three vehicles within it. As you can imagine, Vajrayana is a highly efficient path to enlightenment, but also a risky one. That's why, while you might get away with pursuing the Theravada path without a lama, you really can't do that with Vajrayana.

If you're pursuing Vajrayana on your own, it's just too easy to fool yourself. Just as with any very powerful tool or strong medicine, if you use it incorrectly you can do more harm than good. With less concentrated and powerful medicine, there's less risk of damage (harder to OD on cough drops than on beta-blockers). It's easy to think, "Oh, I've distilled my anger to Mirrorlike Yeshe on this one," when in fact you just haven't. The lama would probably see that and point it out to you, and you would have to take a more honest, though less comfortable, look.

It's a bit like the Sorcerer's Apprentice, playing with something very powerful but not fully knowing how to wield that power. Another example is the story of Icarus, who didn't listen to his father's advice and flew too close to the sun, melting his wings and falling into the sea.

One feature that helps us stabilize ourselves on the Vajrayana path is that, as I've mentioned, it actually contains the other two within it. Especially in the earlier stages, we do many of the same practices that are done in Theravada, though in slightly different styles.

I don't know about you, but I would feel a lot better following the Vajrayana path if there were a way to keep me from going off

track. Fortunately there is a very effective one: the lama. A lama performs several functions similar to those of a typical minister, but also serves as a teacher and guide for students on the particular path to Vajrayana Buddhism.

Of course, you have to make sure you've found a qualified lama. You would want the lama to be well trained in the practices, have actually accomplished the practices, know the theoretical foundation, have sufficiently worked on themselves that their own Buddha Nature is evident, and be proceeding from motives that are pure.

If a lama has all of the above qualifications, is of a lineage you are drawn to, and you feel some connection, then they can be immensely helpful as your spiritual friend and guide.

Since they've worked deeply and intensely with their own Three Poisons and have successfully used proven methods to distill them, they can see when you might be off track, and how you might right yourself. There is no substitute for your regular connection with a live lama. Not all of the teachings are written down, for the very purpose of making sure the student learns from a qualified lama and doesn't proceed into powerful and risky territory unguided. Because of this intention, even the scriptures that teach practices always leave the most important parts out.

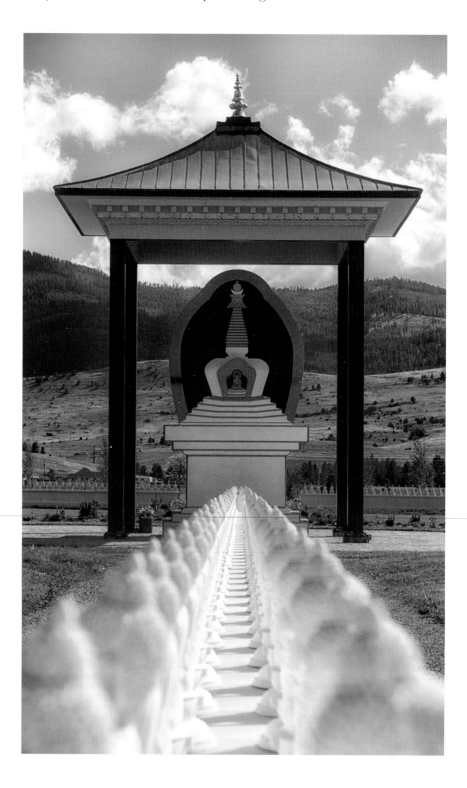

But beyond being a safety net, the lama provides us with a projection screen for *our own Buddha Nature*, which we can't see very well. If we could see it perfectly well, we wouldn't still be here in Samsara.

Yet another benefit we gain from our lama is that, if we truly join our minds with them, we can piggyback onto their level of realization. No kidding. I learned this one by sort of stumbling upon it.

I had been studying with Rinpoche for a few months, doing Guru Yoga, which is the practice of joining one's mind with the lama, in my daily meditation sessions. The next part of my session was the actual meditation. An odd thing was happening during the meditation part. My awareness was far beyond anything I'd experienced before and somehow didn't feel like my own mind that I was so familiar with. It was striking and lovely—very freeing. I called Rinpoche to ask him what that was.

"You've been doing Guru Yoga, right?"

"Yes."

"And you've been connecting with my mind during Guru Yoga?"

"Yes."

"Well, then you're feeling a connection with my level of realization," he said, in a very matter-of-fact way. To him as a Tibetan lama, this was everyday meat and potatoes. To me it was mind-blowing.

Now perhaps you've gotten a taste of the Three Yanas, and where Vajrayana falls within that.

This is a bit of what the Buddha saw. Luckily for us he didn't leave us hanging, but gave us the methods so we can see it for ourselves and reach enlightenment ourselves. With no further delay, let's take a look!

METHODS SO WE CAN
SEE FOR OURSELVES

Checking Our Motivation

Someone once asked the Dalai Lama what the very first thing was
that he did in the morning. He flashed his famous grin and shot
back, "Check motivation!"

In Mahayana and Vajrayana, we have the Two Purposes the
Buddha had: enlightenment for *self* and enlightenment for *others*.
We want our sessions to be imbued with these Two Purposes. In
other words, we want to be sure that our motivation for any practice—anything at all, actually—is compassion, Bodhicitta.

In all of Mahayana and Vajrayana, it's very important to begin
each day, as well as each practice session, by bringing that motivation to mind and making it stronger. If we infuse our practice with
that motivation, the rubber really hits the road. If we don't, the
brilliant, skillful means pretty much do nothing for us. Worse yet,
our efforts won't go toward helping the billions of beings lost in
Samsara, the *vast* majority of whom at this moment don't have the
chance to progress toward enlightenment.

What can someone do toward liberation if they're in a bug

body at this point, for example? And there are infinitely more beings incarnated in bug bodies than human ones. In this lifetime you and I happen to be humans, so we're on the front lines, with countless beings depending on us to make progress. When I'm sleepy in the morning and either feel like skipping the practice or just going through the motions, this thought is often the one that causes me to wake up and invest more of myself in the practice. I'm doing it for everybody else, too.

Student: *What if my motivation isn't so good that morning?*

LT: I say this often, and I'll say it now: A practice session is a "come-as-you-are party."

On any given day, for any given practice, we do what we can at that moment to bring to mind all those beings who are depending on us. Most of them are far worse off than we are but can't do anything about it. Do we want to reach enlightenment just to save our own posterior portions? And never mind about the other poor suckers? Just remembering those other beings (and for the vast majority of my own incarnations, I've been every kind of creature other than human) often helps me. Compassion is a buddha quality because it's evidence that we feel ourselves to be one big awareness. That's why when someone hurts, we feel it.

Then again, if your motivation still isn't so great that morning, be compassionate with *yourself.* You're just a sentient being too, after all. Sometimes we have to "fake it till we make it." The important thing is to show up and do your best. (Woody Allen famously observed that "80% of success is just showing up"; of course, the other 20% is critical, too.)

Fortunately this is only the first ushering-in to the practice. What follows—practices designed to bring forth compassion and mindfulness—will hopefully help. That's why we use all these skillful means, after all!

Now I'd like to ask YOU a question. What's a typical motivation for you, when you sit down to do a session?

Student: *Well, to be honest, it's often that I just want to slow my mind down and get it to focus better.*

LT: Great. Why do you want to do that?

Student: *So I can function better.*

LT: And what will that do? What are you looking for?

Student: *I'm looking to really be there when something good happens—not distracted. To do better work, stay on top of my interactions with my husband and kids.... I mean, I'd like to be more aware, present, and compassionate for everything. I'm especially concerned that I be as compassionate as possible with my kids.*

LT: So if you do better work, and are more aware and compassionate with those around you, what are you hoping will come of that? This may seem like a dumb question, but bear with me.

Student: *Okay. At work I know I could help so many people, if I make the right decisions and am really focused and present. Of course I love my kids and want to be the absolute best for them. And I hope that in the future, they will go out and benefit many people too. A lot of that depends on how I am with them. [Now with tears in her eyes] I guess my motivation, under all that, is really just to benefit beings after all.*

LT: Yes. It was just a little covered over. Now you've really brought it forth. Now, imagine how much more powerful your meditation will be. Then the rubber of your Vajrayana vehicle will really hit the road. So ask yourself these questions, and a couple of questions behind the questions, when you begin your day. And ask yourself again when you begin your meditation session too, if your motivation's not so great right when you wake up.

THE TIBETAN NOSE BLOW

✸ *The Theory*

Okay, Tibetan Nose Blow is not the official name. It's my affection-ate nickname for the practice we do to up our chances of really resting in still, clear, joyful awareness. In Tibetan it's called *Lung Ro Sel*, which is generally translated as "Clearing the Stale Winds (energies)." And no, this is not for clearing the winds from a lower orifice. We're speaking of subtle energies connected to the afflictive emotions—the Three Poisons.

The Tibetans are aware of subtle energy channels that run along either side of the spine, as well as a third one right up the middle. The side ones come up either side of the vertebrae in the neck, over each ear, and out each nostril. I bet you're already begin-ning to see why I call it the Tibetan Nose Blow, but let me continue.

The middle channel is a smoky, dirty blue, and associated with timuk, the poisonous emotion category of ignorance, delusion, stu-por, laziness, narrow-mindedness, and the like. We definitely want to clear *that* before trying to do practice!

The two on either side, as you may have guessed, are the other two passions, or poisonous emotions.

One is anything having to do with our yearning to draw to us the things and experiences that will make us happy. So desire and clinging are classic words used for this category.

The other one involves anything having to do with pushing away the things we *don't* want. Classic words for that category would be aggression, hatred, and aversion.

Desire is a smoky red and aversion a smoky white. You're probably wondering why I'm not telling you which is on which side. I would be happy to, but I simply can't. It's different for different people. It's better if you come to it yourself, but it will still work even if you end up reversing them.

Here's how to tell: We each almost always have a favorite Poison. Some people tend to be very industrious but also tend to get frustrated quickly and have flare-ups of temper. They're obviously the ones who favor aggression/aversion. Another example of someone with an affinity for this Poison—the smoky white channel—would be a very competitive person.

Those of you more partial to desire/longing/clinging might as well admit your tendency and go with the smoky red as your primary channel to clear. This happens to be my personal favorite. I used to hate to admit it, and hoped nobody noticed. Now that I have so much experience in working with all of these poisons in myself, the squeamish, judgmental reactions I used to have about my own tendencies are much, much smaller.

Tulku Sangak Rinpoche has taught that generally women have the red one (desire) on the right and the white one (aversion) on the left, while most men have that reversed. It's really not critical at this stage of training, so there's no need to worry about whether you've got it right. I guarantee you, you have all three, and you'll clear all three pretty well (at least temporarily) by the end of the Clearing of the Stale Winds.

Student: *Every time I try to pick my favorite Poison or passion, I realize I also have the other one. In fact, one leads to the other. I'm angry at my husband because he won't turn off the TV and talk to me. That's because I desire him talking to me. If I weren't so stuck in my small way of thinking about things—ignorance—I wouldn't have a problem with the situation. So just in that one case, I have all three going on. How can I possibly decide?*

LT: You're absolutely right—one does lead to the other. That's part of what makes the Wheel of Samsara keep going around (and why it's not something more linear, like the golf course of Samsara). Of course we all have all three Passions, so this isn't an exclusive decision. We're only talking about picking your favorite, the one that's most basic to your personality—your background color, you might say. Then we'll go ahead and clear *all three*—don't worry!

The Practice

Imagine the primary channel you want to clear on your right side, coming out your right nostril; the other, of course, on your left. And those of you whose favorite is ignorance/laziness/narrow-mindedness can for now just go with your second favorite.

The methods of this exercise block the channels along which the *karmic winds* (karmic energies) run and clear out the neurotic emotions along the main three channels, leaving the energies (winds) of three of the Yeshes to arise in their place. We'll pull the spine really straight, to allow the *yeshe winds* to flow freely. We want those!

Each of the neurotic emotions (Three Poisons) has, at its very core, one of the Yeshes. (In case you're wondering how we get from *Three* Poisons to *Five* Yeshes, I'll tell you. Under the general heading of anger there are two sub-categories: pride and competitiveness/

jealousy. This makes sense to me because both pride and jealousy have an aggressive quality about them.)

Pride and jealousy are associated with the remaining Yeshes, Jewel and Karma. So for this exercise, we'll work with the three major categories of afflictive emotions: the Three Poisons and their associated Yeshes. Later I'll go deeper into the relationship between the Yeshes and the Poisons, but for now I just wanted you to know a little bit about how this exercise works.

Once we've blocked the channels that could hinder our efforts, and cleared the neurotic energies/winds flowing through the others, the yeshe winds can come forth more fully. You can see why you'd want to take half a minute to accomplish *all that*. Everyone I know of who's tried this has found that it really does change their inner experience, in just that short amount of time! Of course it's not a permanent change; that's why we do it before each practice … and then continue on to do the practice itself.

Now you're ready to "assume the position." No, not THAT position! The Seven Point Posture of Vairochana! If you can, get a firm cushion for your rear and sit on the floor or a mat; this helps to elevate the spine, causing it to tend to fall naturally into the right posture. Cross your legs with your feet on top of your legs, as you've all probably seen in yoga class or in most depictions of the Buddha—a yoga position called Full Lotus.

If you're young but not used to this sort of thing, please be gentle with yourself and slowly work your way into this posture over time. If you're older, all the more reason to be gentle with yourself. In time you may be able to do this too, but if not, it's not as though your chances for enlightenment are dashed! If you can sit cross-legged, or even with your feet in front of you, with knees to the side in some way, you can still do this exercise. Many people prop their knees up with small cushions. I hasten to remind you that you only have to hold the position for about half a minute. And, if all else fails, there's always the chair option—you can still reach enlightenment using the chair.

Now that you've woven your legs together, you're going to close some of those pesky channels that tend to carry the more neurotic karmic winds/energies. One of them runs through the base of your fourth finger. With both your hands, you'll make a *vajra fist* by pressing your thumb against the base of your fourth finger and closing the rest of your fingers around it, forming a fist with your thumb inside. The one finger you leave straight is your index finger. You'll need that for covering your nostril.

Now you'll block other hindering, karmic channels that run through the hip joints. You'll curl your vajra fists under so that the backs of them are firmly placed on your legs, almost at the hip joint. Then you'll completely straighten your arms so that they're like poles.

Student: *My arms are too long. There's no WAY I'll ever be able to straighten them.*

LT: I thought the same thing. My arms are so long that most clothes are too short in the sleeves for me. To make matters worse, I'm short-waisted! Still, over time, and with a few helpful pointers, I've been able to hold that position for a half hour at a time. It's worth doing your best with this because you're using your arms to stretch your spine as straight as you possibly can. This allows the yeshe winds to flow more freely—worth the 30 seconds of effort, I'd say!

The Finer Points

To make it easier, you get to rotate the insides of your elbows toward the front. That, and having your seat elevated, will help. So will the slow process of just getting used to it.

Another tip is to let your shoulders come up by your ears. This is actually the official posture. Since a picture is worth a thousand words I've included some for you, if for no other reason than to show you that it's humanly possible!

So that's the Seven Point Posture of Vairochana. Now we're going to blow that smoky stuff out of the three channels in the spine area. Remember, whichever is your favorite—desire (smoky red) or aversion (smoky white)—put that one on the right side, to clear out first. If you're not sure, you can go with the convention that women generally have the red on the right and the white on the left; men the reverse.

Now lift the left fist, drawing a big, slow circle in the air with the index finger. Then place the index finger on your left nostril to block it off. Send that smoky stuff out your right nostril with a long, firm out-breath, ending with a strong push to get the last bit of air out. Imagine that the smoky-looking stuff is the neurotic aspect of the particular Poison, along with the thoughts that come from it. Include sickness on all levels, hindrances of various kinds, and obscurations of our true seeing—anything specific from the Poison you're working with. (Hopefully, nothing else of a more substantial nature will come out; just to make sure, I suggest blowing your nose before you start!)

Now put that fist back on the top of your leg, rotate your elbow as you straighten your arm, and do the same nose-blowing operation on the other side. You alternate the cleansing breaths three times, each time vividly imagining the channels becoming brighter and clearer. By the end, they're perfectly bright and clear, with their true essence flowing through them: the red is Discerning Yeshe and the white is Mirrorlike Yeshe. When you peel away the drama and neuroses and get to their essence, you come to these two Yeshes.

CLEARING ANGER: A PERSONAL STORY

Think of it: That sharp quality that anger has, if you take away the drama and neurosis, is a quality of Mirrorlike Yeshe. Years ago, a friend had repeatedly made plans to get together, then not shown up. I was angry. But insulating against the anger with "fluff" (ignorance, delusion), I believed her excuses. One time, while I was doing a wrathful style practice, this old anger I'd forgotten about came bubbling to the surface. At that moment in meditation, I saw clearly how I was *still* holding a grudge toward that old friend I'd lost contact with many years before.

Had I really harbored anger in some corner of my mind? Unbelievable but true. How embarrassing! I used a powerful technique and the power of a great bodhisattva to clear the anger. What was left was compassion for the person … and crystal clarity about the situation, from her side and mine. I realized that actually we had very little to talk about. I hadn't lived in that place very long and hadn't found many friends, but really she wasn't someone I'd spend time with if there had been other choices. She'd lived there longer and had other choices.

I was able to stop being offended and just accept the truth of the situation. The whole thing was resolved in about twenty minutes. I was no longer in dullness, yet no longer carrying anger. With the help of the practice and my meditational deity (and the lama who brought all of that to me), I was able to drop the drama and come to the essence of Mirrorlike Yeshe, at least in this small way.

Likewise with desire, that emotion that continually says, "No, that's not quite it … I want THIS." Propelled by a longing that rarely has words, we continually chase after happiness, whatever that actually is. Imagine thumbing through a catalog, sometimes called a "wish book." Without the neurosis, as we navigate by the compass of knowing *true joy*, desire boils down to Discerning Yeshe.

If we took this clarifying process to its ultimate end, we would come to the place of ultimate, permanent happiness: Buddhahood. Our longing can actually serve as our compass, if we hold it lightly, peel away the layers of drama, and don't just try to assuage it with quick fixes near at hand.

We've all tried following the quick fixes and dog-earing the pages in our endless wish book, and it only brings us more Samsara. I must confess that I still do this, but after years of practice, I'm much more able to let go of the desire. By using my compass I've gotten better at finding my way to experiences that don't bring me more Samsara, and actually leave me feeling more deeply fed.

Every arrow in the bow of desire
has rushed out in hope
of nearing
Him.

St. Thomas Aquinas

Similarly, if we peel away the layers from the Poison of Ignorance (smoky blue, in the middle) we go from dullness and delusion to the Yeshe of Basic Space (Dharmadatu); from stupor to Timeless Awareness *beyond* words. During that particular time-less half-hour epiphany in college, my mind was awake and aware, but not churning out thoughts. What I saw was beyond concepts. Some mornings, when I'm still in the stupor of sleep, I'm in the less pure, ignorance end of that spectrum.

Back to the Blow by Blow

… so to speak. You've done six exhalations, alternating three on each side. With each out-breath, the once smoky red of desire and white of aggression got clearer and brighter. Now they're perfectly bright and clear red and white. Both fists are back on the tops of your legs with your arms straight, elbows rotated outward. Now you'll blow that smoky blue stuff out of the middle channel—three times out of both nostrils. Again, by the end it's bright, clear azure. What's left to flow through there is the Yeshe of Basic Space, the Timeless Awareness of that ocean of emptiness/awareness that's beyond/before thoughts and words. We go from stupor to wisdom beyond words. How lovely.

Now you gently exhale through the mouth and allow your hands to slide down your legs, unclenching your fists. They can just rest in a free position. The spine goes from firmly straight to a slightly relaxed, supple position—like a marionette hanging from a string. It's still straight, to allow the yeshe winds to flow freely, but with a flexible, floating quality.

Now rest for a moment or two in the new, lovely feeling you're no doubt experiencing. Since you've just cleared those channels that run through your nose, you don't want to stir them up again, so you breathe gently and naturally through your slightly open mouth. After the effort you just went to, why rush ahead? Surely you have another twenty seconds or so to experience this feeling, so relax a bit. Besides, it *feels good*. Sometimes I've got to admit that's been the best part of my practice session!

MORE PROOF OF THE PUDDING

Modern Science and Meditation

"Mindful awareness promotes neural integration."

Contemplative Science—the field that studies the effects of meditation—is new, but it's already surprisingly large, and growing larger. More and more universities across the globe are conducting studies in this area, most of which reveal various marked benefits of meditation. So far, we've mostly had to be satisfied with inklings and tantalizing tidbits gleaned from this or that experiment. In *The Mindful Brain*, psychiatrist, scientist, educator, and meditator Daniel Siegel shows us not just the whether, but also tantalizing hypotheses as to *how*.

Given his background and experience, Siegel is in a particularly good position to put the science, clinical evidence, and meditation experience together in an understandable, sensible, and exceedingly helpful way. I found that not only did most of his hypotheses make sense to me, but if we really accept them, we realize just how powerfully we could use them to change our lives.

In the beginning of the book, Siegel gives us an anatomy lesson on the human brain, takes us with him on his "Meditation Retreat for Scientists," and then weaves back and forth between brain functions and what I'll call mind functions. He makes this distinction, and connection, clear through intriguing statements such as "The mind can actually use the brain to create itself." He shows us how that might work.

Through objective observation—his review of his own and others' laboratory experiments—together with his subjective experience in learning a form of Tranquil Abiding Meditation, Siegel has developed intriguing theories about how our meditation practice changes us both mentally and physically, affecting even how we relate to other people. As with the work of other scientists, the implications are huge.

He brings us current scientific knowledge of what takes place in which parts of the brain, and how these parts work together across regions. He goes on to show how both the regions and the "wires" connecting them can change function and size depending on how we *use* our brains. For most of the history of neuroscience, it was accepted that the brain didn't change after early childhood. But in recent decades, more and more experiments have proved unquestionably that our brains do change throughout our lives.

The term for this newly acknowledged capacity of the brain is *neuroplasticity*, the brain's ability to change how many neurons do which jobs, the number of blood vessels in a particular area, and the nature and number of lines of communication between parts of the brain. All of these changes together can create a whole new map of brain functionality in the same person, over the months and years. The saying "Use it or lose it" applies even on this level!

Neuroplasticity is on the cutting edge of brain science, so there are still many experiments to be done, but many have already clearly shown the benefits of meditation, through functional magnetic resonance imaging (*f*MRI), electroencephalography (EEG), double-blind studies, and other objective methods.

One such study was on attention deficit hyperactivity disorder (ADHD) in both adults and adolescents, many of whom had this disorder in its genetic form. After doing Shamata (Tranquil Abiding) Meditation for just five to fifteen minutes a day for a few months, they showed "marked" improvement! Imagine if those of us without ADHD did the same thing.

Fortunately, we don't have to imagine. Another study compared longtime meditators with "normal" non-meditators and found that the meditators had vastly more capacity to hold their attention on the object of their choice.

But what about those of us who won't be living in a cave for thirty years so we can devote ourselves to daily practice? Will we get any noticeable benefit with much less meditation? A three-month study at the University of California–Davis, worked with subjects with some meditation experience, but not "super-meditators" who had been practicing for decades or meditating extensively every day. The study participants were measured before, during, and after a three-month retreat. Though they couldn't always match the scores of more experienced meditators, they did achieve steady, significant improvement over the three months.

Participants were tested on a variety of attributes, including focus, attention span, and longevity factors that can be measured through blood tests that reflect cellular aging—the wear and tear on the body that can be exacerbated by stress—at the outset of the retreat, halfway through, at the end, and five months after that. Not surprisingly, their beginning scores were the same as those of the control group who weren't on the retreat. Halfway through, though, the meditators had improved markedly on all tests. By the end they were doing even better, while the control group stayed the same. (Before you feel too bad for the control group, be reassured that they got to do the next three-month retreat/study.)

But what happened once the meditators went back to their normal lives? They were tested again after five months, and their changes held! They were still doing shorter daily meditation sessions, but those didn't take up much time in their busy lives.

Let's take a look at one of the key factors: concentration. During the retreat, the meditators were given a difficult though intentionally boring challenge that required intense concentration and comparative analysis. As the retreat continued, the meditators were able to concentrate, and perform, better and better on this task. Again, those improvements held long after the retreat was over. This study suggests that an intensive meditation "boot camp" has immediate, increasing, and lasting benefits.

But what about those of us who don't happen to have three months free? In a much shorter and less intensive study reported in *Time* magazine, scientists at the University of North Carolina at Charlotte found that after only four days of meditation training for just twenty minutes a day, students showed impressive improvement on a variety of cognitive-skills tests. On a timed information-processing test, designed to induce deadline stress, the meditators did significantly better than the controls. On a particularly challenging computer test that measured sustained attention, the brand new meditators did *ten times* better than the control group! Who wants to be in the control group? If schools are supposed to train our minds, why are we not teaching this in all schools? And why wait until university?

There are many other such examples of improvement, in attention span, focus, and "visual discrimination"; many longevity factors, such as relaxation; and even in compassion (yes, they found ways to measure compassion). What are we to make of such brain changes, beginning even after *four days* of short meditation sessions?

For one thing, this means that experience puts its stamp on the brain. This means that, taking advantage of neuroplasticity by carefully setting up a well-designed experience and repeating it again and again, we will increase the size of some of the brain's "real estate,"as well as the blood vessels feeding it and the links to other parts of the brain. In all of the practices in Tibetan Buddhism, we're *choosing* carefully crafted experiences, honed over thousands of years, with huge numbers, designed specifically to make these changes in the best, most efficient way.

Speaking in general terms Siegel says that before learning meditation, most of us take in sensory information from the outside

world, associate that information with similar memories, and then act on that association. For example, if we meet a new person whose face reminds us of a grumpy schoolteacher we had trouble with, we might try to avoid that person, or be more guarded or defensive toward our hapless new acquaintance. Siegel refers to this method of processing as "top-down" because within the geography of the brain, the parts activated in such processes are triggered in a more or less vertical progression.

By contrast, when we use specific parts of the brain associated with what Siegel calls "Executive Attention," characterized by "effortful control" in balance with sensory parts, memories, and others, we operate in more of a wheel shape, with hub (region in charge of Executive Attention and its close relatives), spokes (neural pathways to other regions), and rim (sensory information regions). Siegel shows how brain anatomy corresponds to this process, with the center of Executive Attention at the hub.

In other words, our brain is built to work either way: top-down or like a wheel. You can see how giving voluntary, or "Executive," Attention such a central role can help us be not only more skillful in our responses, but more free—less a prisoner to past experiences, doomed to repeat them again and again. Think of the lady

who reminded us of the grumpy schoolteacher. If we behave badly toward her, how is she likely to behave toward us? Around and around we go.

Repeated meditation, over the course of months or years, increasingly helps us to move from the vertical, knee-jerk process to the more intentional, free, and resourceful wheel process.

Contemplative Science goes on to show that we *sustain* changes catalyzed by meditation even after we get up off the cushion. Once the pathways and processes are set, the new way of functioning becomes the "default" way of dealing with all experience. The old synapses (pathways) gradually diminish, some even disappearing after months and years of disuse. Through repeated use, the new ones go from footpaths, to streets, to thoroughfares.

Many experiments have shown that the techniques of Tibetan Buddhism help us put just the right paths between just the right parts of the brain, and balance them in just the right way, so that we can let go of knee-jerk reactions and have compassionate, balanced, resourceful, and constructive responses to experiences—and people—that come our way.

In his book, Siegel maps all this out in detail, citing some of the studies on Tibetan Buddhist meditators. I've included some others here as well. Though I don't agree with all of Siegel's hypotheses, I have to say that I've found many of them (and those of Contemplative Science) to be true for me, as well as for most of my students. Speaking from their subjective experience, almost all of my students have reported being better able to handle painful experiences with less stress, and having more mastery over challenging interactions with others. They also report a generally heightened sense of well-being, with greater capacity for love, joy, and compassion. I would report the same for myself.

But the benefit of the practices doesn't stop there. The knee-jerk mental process also produces endless chatter. Anyone who's spent ten minutes trying to meditate knows that! Siegel takes us with him on his first meditation retreat, which was was the mental equivalent of going from couch potato to marathon boot camp. At first he went "a little stir-crazy," finding the long sessions weird and uncomfortable.

After a huge inner struggle, he was soon able to drop that internal conversation for at least a few minutes, or the duration of a meditation session. Then this newfound clarity and focus began to persist even on breaks between sessions. He was now free to really *feel* the cool breeze on his face, really *see* the forest around him: free to allow the heart-rending beauty of the moment to penetrate him. The first time that happened fully, he burst into tears.

Connecting

Not only have I spent most of my life separated from experience by my internal monologue, I've dampened my emotions to protect myself from feeling. When I was about thirteen, I thought, "If I could just feel the good things in life and not feel the bad, wouldn't that be great?" After numbing myself till my life was in black and white, I realized I was living in a state of mild depression. Everything was gray and two-dimensional—like I was looking at life instead of actually living. I would go to the mountains and only experience the beauty and vastness as though I were sipping from a waterfall through a straw. The exquisite mountain was fully there, but I wasn't.

Through body-centered psychotherapy, I began to feel everything more fully again. Through Tibetan meditation practices, I've been able to let go of the unhappy feelings—let go of all lingering thoughts/feelings from the past, conjecture about the future—so that I can REALLY feel what's happening in the moment. As the saying goes, "God is here; where are you?"

When I'm having a difficult interaction with someone, I'm more able to manage my responses and freer to respond more kindly, resourcefully, and ultimately successfully. I'm by no means perfect, but the vast improvement is obvious to me as well as others who have known me for a long time.

But there's yet another experience that comes with letting go of the top-down way of processing life. We're no longer prisoners of the self we thought we were. Once we're operating more from the hub of the wheel, we're not just a composite of memories and habitual reactions. Those memories are there, but with hours of meditation experience, we don't identify so tightly with those memories and habitual patterns. We're able to open up to what the Contemplative Scientists are calling the *ipseity* sense of ourselves, a more basic sense of being that Siegel likens to the Theravada Buddhist term "bare awareness." Perhaps pointing at the same phenomenon, Thich Naht Hanh, a famous Vietnamese Zen master, refers to "Interbeing."

In my experience, I drop or suspend my personality to an extent, and am able to sink to a more profound level beneath it, which I simply call awareness. Because I have this awareness in common with everyone else, this helps immensely with my ability to join with others. I feel joined with all things, all creations within the one great awareness. It's much easier to be moral—natural, really—when coming from this place. Just as when I stub my toe, my whole self experiences it, from the point of view of "me" being the whole ocean, when one being suffers, I suffer too.

In meditation I often feel free of my usual sense of self, but it's more than that. I feel that my awareness goes beyond my skin. Siegel invented the term *transpirational integration*, meaning that as the different regions of the brain relate in this balanced way, there is a sense of "breathing across" the different regions. This can extend into a breathing across from one human to another, one human to all creation.

So this psychiatrist has perhaps begun to point at *how*, in the brain, we're able to *feel* this universal truth that's been expressed for ages, from Sufi poetry to Hildegard von Bingen's revelations, to the mystics of all religions. In Buddhism we say that without the constructed self in the way, we can experience the one vast awareness that I'm calling *Buddha Mind*. There is no more immediate, no truer perception of reality than that. And nothing more satisfying and joyful. It's the ultimate experience of *coming home.*

So if your goal is to be healthier, smarter, better (i.e., more compassionate and skillful), and ultimately happier, you now know that this set of methods is scientifically endorsed!

Instructional video for this practice is available at www.namchak.org

TRANQUIL ABIDING

Shamata

There are a few things I really like about *Shamata*, translated from Sanskrit as "Tranquil Stillness," or "Peaceful Abiding." I like the term *Tranquil Abiding*, because when we Westerners start doing this practice, we tend to demand that our minds suddenly be still. We think meditation means sitting there and thinking of nothing for a half hour. The emphasis for me, though, is the tranquility of the experience. *Shiney*, the Tibetan term for Shamata, literally means "Tranquil Abiding."

I also like how very restful Shamata can be, as its name implies. We tend to spend all day relating to people and things outside ourselves. Even if we aren't actively relating to them *out there*, we're thinking about them *inside* ourselves, in between, in our thoughts and feelings. Even at night, in our dreams, our minds are busy. Even when we finally get to sit on the beach. Even between lifetimes.

We've chased after thoughts, following them with the next thoughts, following those with words and actions ... for an eternity. Wouldn't it be nice to take a break from making these movies all the time? To take a REAL break, and just *rest*? I get exhausted just at the thought of how long I've been ceaselessly dashing around, mentally or physically. We all need a vacation, right? Well, I take a *real* one every day—in my morning practice session!

And what makes it especially nice is that I get to *officially* do nothing and be *virtuous* in the bargain! No answering the phone, no thinking about work, no deciding what to do about dinner, no solving the vexing problems in my life—whew! No wonder doctors recommend forms of meditation for high blood pressure. I know some women who do it just to slow the aging process. Scientists have found that meditation boosts the immune system for many hours afterward.

And because I don't have to do or think about anything on the outside during Shamata, I can turn the lens inward, at last. I can just sit with my mind. In doing this simple practice, I've learned more about the true nature of my mind and how it works than in all my years of studying psychology. For all the reasons the Buddha has taught us, we might as well know what's really going on in there, so we can go about straightening it out ... or even just to *know*. (As the New Testament says, "You shall know the truth, and the truth shall make you free.")

I don't know about you but I'm *curious*—fascinated, even. And if I run into something I want to change, I have the methods to do it. But during Tranquil Abiding, we don't even have to direct our thoughts or come up with diagnoses and remedies. That comes in other practices. Here we just see them and remain, well, tranquilly abiding. After all this running around, reacting to outer phenomena all our lives (and countless others), we haven't ever just sat with our minds and observed them. What better way to learn the nature of our minds? If we want to refine something, we first need to know the nature of the thing.

As I've said, many modern people think we have to make our

minds stop thoughts altogether during meditation. But the brain is, among other things, a thinking machine. It's okay to leave the machine on and let thoughts come and go. The problem comes when we chase after these thoughts and make whole movies about them. *That is the cause of our suffering.* The Buddha saw exactly how that works, and I've shared some of his explanation. As you sit in Shiney you'll see those dynamics in action, for yourself.

I've noticed a big catch-22 with these practices. We're using the impure mind to work on the mind. So if the tool is imperfect, won't the results be imperfect? That's why we begin with Shamata. We need to refine the tool. Meanwhile, we will already begin, in the process, to get to know the nature of our minds.

There's another catch-22, and at one point I asked Rinpoche about it. Many of the practice texts say that if you do a practice perfectly, and your mind doesn't waver for a moment, and you perceive everything in just the right, enlightened way, you can reach enlightenment by doing that practice. But if I could do the practice that way, I'd already *be* enlightened, and I wouldn't need to do the practice! I pointed this out to Rinpoche, who smiled, knowing all about this, and said, "We keep on doing the practice, and little by little, it will distill our minds so that we will reach the goal after all."

There's yet another important reason for doing Tranquil Abiding. I think we'd all like to be better able to focus our minds on something and have it stay there. We can all do it sometimes, for a short time, but what if your mind became more dependably really peaceful and stable? I'm not talking about sinking into a stupor; quite the contrary. When we're doing good Shamata our minds are resting in their true state, which is bright, clear, and vivid. Wouldn't *that* be a nice way to start or end the day—resting in clear, vivid awareness?

I've always wanted to fully experience a beautiful moment, like the sun painting the clouds with pastel light at sunset. But my mind was so constantly lost in its movies that I could never be fully there;

now I can. Of course the sunset is fully available to you. With some practice at this technique you can fully be there for it, too.

When we do Shamata long term, our minds become more supple, even as they become more stable. This is not a rigid practice; it's a very gentle one. It wouldn't be very restful if it were rigid, would it? Masters who have done a lot of this and other practices for years find that they need very little sleep. It seems that the rejuvenating effects of such practices are more efficient than normal sleep. Who wouldn't like *that* fringe benefit?

Yet another reason to do Shamata—and this one is essential—is that without that ability to put our mind on something and have it stay there, how can we get any serious benefit from the other practices? If our minds can't stay on the mantra or the visualization, no matter how brilliantly the practice is engineered, it can't do us much good. That's why, even though this is the main practice of Theravada (School of the Ancient Ones), we also begin with this practice in Vajrayana. As you can probably see, it's foundational. Sure, we'll go on to build the walls and the roof, but first let's lay a good foundation so the house really serves us well.

The Actual Practice of Tranquil Abiding— A Brief Introduction

Now that you've brought forward your Bodhicitta motivation and done the Tibetan Nose Blow, you're in a *much* better frame of mind to do this practice.

Now you can begin the main part. Sit with your back in that supple-yet-straight position. Your pelvis is rotated slightly forward, with your lower belly hanging forward a bit. If you can sit cross-legged on a firm cushion, that's ideal. Almost cross-legged, with one foot in front, is also good. If not, a chair with a firm seat is fine too. In that case I'd recommend a small, firm, wide cushion at the small of your back. There are lots of orthopedic back support gadgets out there that work well. You could give them a try.

Another option that I happen to be fond of, because of a hip problem, is what I call the "knees-up" position. I sometimes alternate it with the cross-legged position. Sitting on the floor on a firm cushion, you put your feet together and your knees up. You can wrap your arms around your knees and clasp your hands together for support. For this position, I like to use the *gom tak*, a Tibetan meditation belt. It's a band of felt that wraps around your back, as well as your knees. Generally it's nearly four inches wide; the length depends on your size. You can buy these from some Dharma stores online (ours, for one!). Some students have simply used a very large, wide belt.

Whichever position you choose, the main point is that your back has to be straight, without strain.

Your shoulders should be back. Your hands are typically folded, one on top of the other, palms facing up, in your lap. If that gets to be hard on your shoulders (I tend to slump, so I'm in this category), you can let your hands rest farther down each leg, close to the knees. I have my palms facing down, but Rinpoche doesn't seem to be too strict on this point.

If you're a marionette hanging from the ceiling, with the string coming out the top/back of your head, your chin naturally comes down a bit. As a matter of fact, your jaw is slack and slightly open, village idiot–style. Your teeth and lips don't quite meet, and you're breathing very gently through your mouth. (After clearing our nostrils through Lung Ro Sel, a.k.a. the Tibetan Nose Blow, we don't want to stir the karmic winds up again!) The tip of your tongue just touches the place where your upper teeth meet the roof of your mouth.

Your eyes are in a downward gaze, only half open. Your breath wafts in through your mouth and your belly swells as it comes in—like filling a wineskin—filling from bottom to top. On the out-breath, you reverse the process, letting the air out from top to bottom.

✦ Some Shamata Tips

Student: *In other meditation classes I've learned to close my eyes in medita-tion. I like that. Can I just go ahead and close my eyes?*

LT: Rinpoche has taught me from his lineage, and there will be all kinds of differences in technique from lineage to lineage. One reason to have the eyes half-open is that when they're closed we can more easily go off on some fantasy or train of thought. We're also more likely to settle into a stupor or even nod off to sleep. We don't want to fall into either mental meanderings or stagna-tion in our practice. We tend to go from one to the other in life, and we're trying to do something quite different here. As Mingyur Rinpoche would put it, the key is to ... *rest, but not get lost.*

We're going for ... *vivid, joyful stillness.*

Rinpoche has taught me to keep my eyes open to let the light in. That seems to help achieve that vivid, joyful stillness. As Ram Dass famously advised us ...

Be ... here ... now.

Rinpoche has also pointed out that the aim of Vajrayana is to join the state achieved in prac-tice with everyday life. We're laying that founda-tion when we keep our eyes a bit open, allowing the apparitions of this world to remain within our eyesight, while we rest our minds in the underlying reality. Eventually we want to master joining both reali-ties—the ocean and its waves, the Two Truths—in our view. He has said that keeping the eyes open is also better preparation for Dzogchen, the highest level in Tibetan Buddhism.

Be ... here ... now.

Student: *Is it okay to play background music while I do Shamata?*

LT: Alas, no. Though it could be pleasant, it would detract from this particular mind training you're pursuing.

Student: *I can sit cross-legged on a cush-ion, which I'd like to do, but after a while my foot falls asleep.*

LT: Many of us have had that problem. Me too. A few tips can make a big difference. One is to make sure your cushion is very firm. If you're sinking into your cushion, it's much more likely you'll cut off your blood supply. The other advice is to sit right on your sit-bones, moving the, er, flesh out of the way as you sit down. Then you're moving the blood vessels out of the way, too. Also, unlike the Theravada version of this, if you need to move in the middle of your session because your foot is falling asleep, you may. At that point you might want to switch to the knees-up position.

Now we'll do twenty-one breaths as a deeper ushering-in to the session. Again, the air floats gently through our mouths, swelling our lower bellies first. Then it fills the rest of our trunks. We pause as long as is comfortable, then exhale. Gentle pause again. That's one. Continue that way till you've done twenty-one of those. I like to use my mala to count. I put a marker bead at #21 on my mala, then go to the large "guru bead," so I don't have to count to get to it every time. You can always repeat the twenty-one breaths anytime during your session.

Student: *I've noticed many meditation traditions have us focus on our breath. What's the reason for this?*

LT: There are probably several, and the short answer is, I don't know. I do know from personal experience that it helps me to settle into a more alert yet calm state, with a minimum of distraction—relatively speaking!

When I looked up *inspiration* in the *Oxford English Dictionary*, it defined it in two ways. One was "inhalation"; the other, "divine influence." Why would those two meanings be embedded in our language? What unconscious understanding let us see those as related? We also speak of the "breath of life," not referring just to a biological need for oxygen.

When we practice Shamata, we're spending a few minutes out of the twenty-four hours of breathing we do in a day being *aware* of—*present* for—our taking in the divine and being affected and

sutained by it. What better foundation for mindfulness practice? What better ushering-in to the tranquil state we're seeking?

Clearing the Stale Winds bases its methodology on the understanding that thoughts and emotions ride the breath. Using the breath, we clear away those unwanted thoughts and emotions. Now we let the breath come in, naturally, tranquilly, while focusing our intention and attention on the breath itself. This makes sense to me.

Harking back to *The Mindful Brain*, Siegel notes that our breathing is operated by both the automatic and intentional parts of our nervous systems; unconscious and conscious; body and mind. How interesting, to sit on that cusp while practicing mindfulness and tranquility.

Shamata: The Main Event

Now we're really into the main part. In the first months you'll want to use an "object of support," as it's called. Think of it as training wheels. I sure appreciated them when I was learning to ride a bike! As you practice, have a picture or statue of an enlightened being in your line of sight (remember: your eyes aren't closed!). Examples would be the Buddha Shakyamuni, the founder of Buddhism. Another would be Guru Rinpoche, who brought Vajrayana Buddhism to Tibet, and reached full Buddhahood himself. Another would be his consort, Yeshe Tsogyal, and another would be their Great Mother figure, Green Tara, or any of the Twenty-One Taras that emanate from her, for that matter. Remember our discussion on the power of images—archetypal ones, in particular.

In case you don't happen to have such an image handy, I've included one in this packet. It's Vajradhara, which according to the Nyingma tradition, is the Sambhogakaya (the archetypal) level form of the Primordial Buddha. It's in *yab-yum*, which means "in both its male and female forms, in union." This symbolizes the union of the realized masculine and feminine principles, awareness/emptiness, wisdom/skillful means, wisdom/compassion, and many others.

I do find it beautiful and evocative. To me they're like the original father and mother—the ones we all wish we'd had, but we had neurotic sentient beings for parents instead (of course, they had us—neurotic sentient beings—for kids, so it evens out). I love my parents, but of course they're imperfect. Beholding the pure forms evokes something very healing for me. If you're going to stare at something for hours, it might as well be beautiful, evocative, and inspiring.

New science has found that images registered in the retina go immediately to the amygdala, an almond-sized/shaped part of our brain. The amygdala is sometimes likened to an orchestra conductor. Built for survival, it instantly sends its interpreted messages to whatever parts of the brain it's programmed to send them to. Since survival trumps everything else, so do the messages of the amygdala.

For example, we're walking down a forest path. Suddenly our heart starts to pound and we jump to the side. Only later do we realize we'd seen a stick out of the corner of our eye. The amygdala associated the twisted, oblong shape with "snake" and sent messages to the heart and legs before our conscious mind in the cerebral cortex had a word to say about it. As scientific studies have shown, it hadn't even gotten the message yet. Later we can take the time to decide if it's really a snake and think about what to do. Our survival programming gives us the luxury of that time, which in hunter-gatherer days meant life or death.

The Tibetans may not have known about the amygdala, but they sure understood the immediacy of imagery, and how it engages all levels, conscious and unconscious. Jung did extensive experiments on association and proved that our brains work almost entirely on association. He based many of his theories on that knowledge.

One student *insisted* on meditating on a penny that he'd whip out of his pocket and toss on the ground in front of him. Even after I'd explained why an enlightened being might be a tad more inspiring, he stuck with his penny as his meditative support. In fact he became insistent. Oh, well. I practiced patience. It was his choice, after all. Many months went by, until he announced one night that he couldn't imagine why he'd want to meditate on money. For many years he'd been dedicated to a life free from worrying about money. Why meditate on a penny—especially when he was having some hard times financially. Why, indeed? It would have been un-Buddhist to say "I told you so." So I didn't.

After you've taken your twenty-one breaths, keep your gaze steadily resting on the image in front of you.

THOUGHT EXPERIMENT

To give yourself a sense of how you're affected by imagery, I invite you to take a moment to be your own scientist. Please stop and remember a scary scene in a movie. Maybe a malevolent person or creature was sneaking up behind our hero or heroine. How did you feel in that moment? Most of us feel anxious, our hearts beating faster, our breath short, eyes wide, almost as if it were happening to us in real life. Now zero in on your memory of the "bad guy's" face. Do you feel warm and fuzzy? I doubt it. What are you feeling?

Now rest your gaze on the face of Guru Rinpoche or White Tara. What qualities do you see there? What feelings arise in you? Please jot them down.

All of these—the "bad guy," Guru Rinpoche, White Tara—are archetypal images that we tend to associate with certain qualities and that tend to evoke corresponding feelings. Why not use the positive images to help us rouse the positive thoughts and feelings we want to cultivate in our lives? Scientists are only just now beginning to discover the effects of imagery throughout the depths and

breadth of the brain. Tibetan practices, in particular, make use of this phenomenon in a highly refined way. So, as Tibetan Buddhists have known for centuries and as modern scientists are also discovering, there are good reasons for us to use an image of an enlightened being in our practice. Perhaps in this little experiment, you've begun to get an inkling.

Now What?

Well, here you are, having "assumed the position" for Tranquil Abiding, *looking like* a buddha, and hopefully *breathing* like a buddha, while looking *at* a buddha.

The main point of the whole exercise is what you do with your *mind*. The answer? Nothing.

Rest in your truly natural state: joyful, heartful, alive, and relaxed. That's it. I'm not kidding. Oh, if only our minds would do that for a nice, long time!

Mind in Agitated State

Once, long ago, a man received a wonderful present from a master: a magical monkey that could do anything the man asked of it. Well, of course he was thrilled! He took the monkey along with him and asked it to do all sorts of useful things. In no time at all, it would finish each task and come running back for the next order. The man had him build him a palatial house. In no time at all, the monkey had finished it. Now our friend was *really* thrilled. What's not to like?

The man went to bed for the night and found out. The monkey kept pestering him, "NOW what do you want me to do? What next?" The man could never rest, ever! Day and night the monkey hounded him with requests for more work, which it finished in no time. Then it was back for more.

At his wits' end, the man went back to the master. "Help! You've *got* to give me a way to deal with this monkey so that it doesn't keep on bothering me day and night! What can you do?!"

The master gave him one curly hair. He intoned, "Have the monkey make the hair go straight." The master demonstrated pulling the hair straight. As soon as he let go, the hair bounced back to its former shape. That was it. The man took the hair and gave it to the monkey, ordering it to make the hair straight. The monkey sat down, fully focused on the little hair. He pulled it straight. It bounced back. He pulled it again. It bounced back again. So it went for about a minute. The man raced to his bed and gratefully passed out.

This story was from the days before the hair product Curl Free.

Many Buddhists refer to the "monkey mind," and now you know why. Our discursive mind is like the mind of that monkey: it serves us well but never gives us a moment's rest. Even at night we're living out dramas and working out problems in our dreams. Great masters who rest in the clear light of basic awareness need very little sleep—and I daresay they get more rest!

Our meditative support acts like the curly hair. After lifetimes of busily dashing after thoughts, if we ask the mind to suddenly "take five," how could it possibly do that? If we ask a puppy to do a "down-stay" for an hour in the first lesson, we're going to have a very unhappy puppy and owner. It simply ain't gonna happen.

We'd do well to give it a bone to chew on. It still won't stay for an hour, but it'll stay for a bit. I don't know of any Theravada or Mahayana Lineages that use an image as a meditative support in the way that we do, but I like the fact that Vajrayana does, in the beginning. As I've tried one after another Vajrayana practice, I've found these practices very realistic in meeting our minds as they are NOW. From that starting point, the practices lead us to loftier, more rarified states. The higher the level of practice, the stronger the medicine, until you're experiencing some really amazing things. Most important, your mind has really changed. If we try to start at the lofty places, though, the mind will be like that fidgety untrained puppy being asked to do a "down-stay" for an hour.

Remember that you're not expected to sit there and think of nothing for the whole time. Again, that's not realistic. But many Westerners beginning meditation do make this mistake, drive themselves crazy in the attempt, and get discouraged and/or give up. If as we meditate, thoughts arise and fall away, like waves in the ocean, no problem. That's reality. Empty awareness gives rise to appearances, and thoughts are a kind of appearance. If we could let well enough alone … we wouldn't be in this mess of a movie we call Samsara. The Buddha also saw the appearances, but he didn't have to do or think anything about them, so he could let them be.

But rarely can we let well enough alone. Because we identify with one apparition, "me," ego, we have a vested interest in following the course of this movie, in which we are both audience and the main character.

SIGNING UP FOR SAMSARA BY THE NANOSECOND

A thought arises and we grab hold of it.

We generate another thought in response to that one, perhaps embellishing our thought in pursuit of something we desire, or perhaps changing the subject in an effort to push away an unwanted experience.

And on and on and on it goes, one thought tumbling after another, all spurred on by "needs" of our afflictive emotions. We want to attract this thing we're thinking of, and push away that other thing.

All those internal conversations you have going on, oh, once in a while. The endless problem solving, as you try to figure out how you can get that promotion, push that difficult person out of your way, make someone like you back, etc., etc., etc.—*that's* not letting well enough alone. That's not Tranquil Abiding. We sign up for Samsara every moment, involved with the movie, jumping in and starring in it, trying to produce, direct, rescript, and recast it as it flows by. We could stop at any frame, but we don't even notice that there are separate frames, or even that it's a movie.

Let's look at this chain reaction in slow motion. You're sitting there, meditating, breathing and gazing peacefully. The thought of your manager at work pops up. Yesterday she told you she didn't like your clever idea. You see her face in your mind's eye. You hear her dismissive tone. NOW is the moment you could simply be aware of that thought and let it pass. But in a less-than-mindful moment, with frustration (the little brother of aversion/aggression) in your heart, you jump to the next link in the chain reaction. You think of what you'd say back to her, trying different sentences, imagining how she responds. Then you decide maybe it would be better to go over her head and tell her manager or to get your fellow workers to join you in putting your idea forward. The more you spin these scenarios, the more agitated, and less peaceful, you feel.

You see how this plays out: now you've got a whole movie going on, and you're the star. And there is nothing tranquil or abiding about this production.

And maybe, at some point in your revved-up agitation, you remember: Oh, yeah, I was meditating.

The drama started not with the image and words of your man-ager, actually, but with your *following after that thought*. And in that moment you went from peace to Samsara. This is how we sign up for Samsara every minute, every day.

We commonly say, "You made me mad." Well, Rinpoche prob-ably felt like saying that to the guards when he first got to prison. But then he learned that, whatever the guards did or whatever situ-ation he was in, *his own reaction was quite another thing*. This uncoupling of outer goings-on from our reactions to them is key to our finding peace. If we're dependent on everything being just right in our outer world, it's going to be a long wait (and by "long," I mean "infinite"), so we'll never find happiness. Gaining the ability to respond as we wish to is the only way I can imagine to be happy all the time. It's also the way to true freedom.

If we don't have any personal (ego) stake in what happens when

a face and words pop up, then they very quickly vanish, without any drama. In Vajrayana they sometimes speak of a thief coming to an empty house. There's no point in staying. So if we become a dispassionate observer—not numbed out but simply without indulging in that "personal stake"—these thoughts, appearances, even feelings can come and go in an endless flow, and we haven't lost our seat. Under these circumstances, gradually the flow of thoughts will naturally slow down. We can experience the true nature of our minds, see to the depths, only once the waters have been stilled.

Even in the early stages of Shamata practice, I found I could experience a bit of stillness in the pause between breaths. I found I would lengthen that pause a little, to savor that lovely stillness. You might try that yourself, without pushing or making a big effort out of it. Just a little pause.

In the gap between two thoughts,
Thought-free wakefulness manifests unceasingly.
—MILAREPA

YOUR MIND WORKING ON YOUR MIND—
CATCH-22? A LITTLE.

At this point, let's face it: we can't do pure Tranquil Abiding very well or very long, even if we sit in the proper position and breathe the proper breaths. It's going to take time, but if you're gentle and consistent in training that puppy of a mind, you'll see progress. Most of my students were very discouraged at the beginning, and thought they were getting nowhere. And as you remember, I gave up altogether myself at one point, thinking the same thing.

But after a few months, most of them reported that friends, relatives, and coworkers were asking them what they were doing differently. They'd changed for the better, and people had noticed. So the Shamata Project isn't the only proof in the pudding. Most meditation classes are the proving grounds. After so many millennia, there must be a reason why people in Asia are still spending so much time doing it, and why many of us in the West have taken it up.

After two or three months in my weekly seminar, one student's sister suddenly died. Everyone at the funeral was grief-stricken. After she returned, the student told me, "Of course I was very sad, and will miss my sister very much. But I now had a way to work with my mind around the loss. I looked at the suffering people around me and thought, 'How are THEY going to deal with this?' I don't know how *I* could've dealt with it before doing this practice."

Rinpoche had to assure me again and again that it is fine to have thoughts arise. *Just so long as we don't grasp at or follow after them.* He gave the analogy of a still pond, perfectly reflecting the sky.

Clouds will pass by from time to time, reflected in the pond. Then they pass on, and the pond is once again reflecting blue sky. Then another cloud and another, and so on. The pond doesn't leave its place to go chasing after this or that cloud. Our mind can be like that pond.

One metaphor I've come up with over the years is a rope passing across my open hand. I can either grab hold of the rope and get pulled off my seat, or I let it pass through, registering the simple image and feeling of the rope as it passes, but having no particular dramas around it, no need to grab on to it. Once it passes on, no feeling of the rope.

> *Though the view should be as vast as the sky, keep your conduct as fine as barley flour.*
> —GURU RINPOCHE

Over time I became more and more able to let the thoughts pass through. Whenever I noticed that I had been chasing a train of thought, I was able to make a *decision* to let it go, saying, "I don't have to think about that right now." What a relief! I really liked the open, buoyant feeling of not having to pursue a thought, of taking a vacation *in that very moment*. After some time, I developed that habit strongly enough that I am now able to do the same thing during the course of the day, in the moment.

As Guru Rinpoche tells us, "Though the view should be as vast as the sky, keep your conduct as fine as barley flour."

People think meditation happens by the minute or hour, but it happens moment by moment.

Unrealistic Expectations
(or, I Want Patience, and I Want It Now!)

As we've said, we can't have ridiculous, unrealistic expectations. If a teacher yells at a child when they do something they've always done before, the teacher is not going to have a very good student. It will actually take much longer to train that child, if at all, and both teacher and student will be absolutely miserable in the process.

Because the unconscious mind is much bigger and stronger than the conscious mind, I don't see how you can ever beat it into submission by saying, "Oh, I'm a lousy meditator. Look, I screwed up AGAIN!" Anyone who's ever tried to diet knows you can't bully the subconscious. It will win in the end. I've given up dieting and started really listening to what (and how much) my body actually wants. I've weighed about twenty pounds less for decades since.

Maybe our problem is that we think we should already be able to do this Shamata thing. It reminds me of my son: a week before his first piano lesson he urgently asked me to teach him some piano. I said, "But you're just about to start taking lessons." After increasingly insistent requests and my same answer, he finally replied, "But that's WHY I need you to teach me—quick, before I have to play at that first lesson!" He thought he already had to know how to play piano. I assured him that the teacher was expecting him to know nothing and was fully prepared to start teaching him from the beginning. So allow yourself to be a rank beginner! Even if you've tried this before, you might as well allow yourself to have the wandering mind of a sentient being. (I'll bet you still are one.) These practices are *designed* to start where we are and go from there.

Another problem is that while we're yelling at ourselves, we're definitely not doing Tranquil Abiding! The key to enlightenment is going beyond ego identification. But in the process of bawling ourselves out, we're producing a very dramatic movie in our minds … with ourselves as the star. This is the opposite of the object of the exercise.

As Westerners, and this is perhaps particularly true for Americans, we focus on the individual: self-sufficiency, self-reliance, individual rights, rugged individualism. These are all powerful, and often positive and constructive concepts.

But if we focus only on our individual selves, we are also cultivating isolation, detachment, and a profoundly limited sense of the fundamental unity of all reality. A good medicine for this self-limiting loneliness would be to cultivate a new habit of being every time you sit down to meditate. You drop the drama that you're the star of (and dare I mention it? the *author*). You take a break from chasing after what you "need" and running from what is "bad" for you. You expand your definition of "I" (ego) to include all and everything, at least for a little while.

✺ *When We Realize We've Been Following a Thought*

As we've noted, many modern people mentally beat themselves up just for *having* a train of thought and become so frustrated, and discouraged, that they can't sustain a full session of Tranquil Abiding.

In fact, Rinpoche *recommended* that I do meditation in short mini-sessions, meaning from moment to moment. No, not getting up and fixing breakfast! When we notice that we've been following a train of thought, at that moment—in that mini-session—we're more aware than we've been for most of our life! Maybe many lives. That moment of noticing the movie is something to celebrate! If we praise the puppy whenever it does what we want, it will tend to do it more and more. Great! (One of the most useful insights of behavioral psychology, particularly the strand pioneered by B. F. Skinner, is that it is productive to reward the behavior we're looking for, but it is *not* productive to punish unwanted behavior, which should, instead, just be ignored.)

The moment we recognize we've been following a thought and we let it go—the moment of remembering (until we forget, and start making another movie)—marks the end of this mini-session

I'm speaking of. Then we settle back into that calm, bright, whole-ocean state. This marks the beginning of the next mini-session.

We can do many of these mini-sessions in one sitting (and, over time, they will get less "mini" as we do this practice). As a matter of fact, if we've done a lot of these, we've had a lot of moments of mindfulness, which is a great thing! So the arising of thoughts is actually an opportunity—grist for the mill of awakening.

In that moment when we've *realized*, "Oh, I've just been following a train of thought," we have a great *opportunity*. We can

choose to take a vacation from that drama and rest in buoyant, simple awareness. In *that instant* we're really doing Tranquil Abiding. We probably can't stay in that state for more than a few moments, in the beginning, but that's okay. Contrary to popular belief, it's not how *long* we stay in that state, but how *often*, particularly in the beginning. Actually, Rinpoche has said that the more often we drop freshly into that state, the more we're having that alive, true experience. There is little chance for stagnation if we're constantly renewing that state.

The word in Tibetan for meditate, *gom*, means a few different things. Depending on the spelling it can mean "meditate," "visualize," or "completely familiarize." The connotation of the last meaning is that we step onto this place with the familiarity of having experienced it again and again so that we have utter confidence. What a concept!

People sometimes think if they have a moment of revelation or clarity, that they've arrived. But have they really? Have they done more than take a peek? If they're still bumbling around, sowing seeds of disaster just as before, despite that revelatory experience, I'd say they might want to spend some *time* there—not just pass through on a single visit or two, and then talk about it, but take up residence there. It's the difference between taking a two-hour tour of Paris and moving there to live; you're not a Parisian just because you saw the Eiffel Tower from a tour bus. Enlightenment is a long, transformational process. The glimpses are crucial, but they're not the end, or the whole.

One time at a presentation by a panel of leaders from various faiths, a woman from the audience said that she'd had a near-death experience and since then had acquired clairvoyance and other amazing abilities. She'd been told that she was enlightened and was wondering if it was true. One panelist after another squirmed, danced around the question, and said a lot of nothing. The last panelist was Chagdüd Tulku, a Tibetan lama. He asked her three simple questions: "Do you ever feel lazy?" "Yes." "Do you ever feel desire or longing?" "Sure." "Do you ever feel angry?" "Well, yeah." "Then you're not enlightened."

Agitation, Perhaps Our Most Popular Pitfall

At least in the West, it seems.

The mind often falls into two states: agitation or dullness, mind racing around or else sunk in a stupor. Neither feels very good, and neither is what we're looking for here. Particularly in modern times—when we race around in planes, trains, and automobiles, and we work on computers that measure time in nanoseconds, and we watch images flash by on TV screens—our minds are all too often in a state of agitation, especially as we try to "multitask," as though it were an achievement to be doing more and more things simultaneously with less and less sustained and deep attentiveness. We dash from thought to thought, quite often getting nowhere fast (like the old joke: "We're lost, but we're making good time!"). I love the title of a book on meditation retreat: *Don't Just Do Something, Sit There*, by Sylvia Boorstein.

What do we do if we find ourselves in such a state? Much of the above advice and insight help you to understand and deal with it. We can also rest our gaze a bit farther down; gaze at the lower part of the buddha in front of you. Yet another time-honored technique that sometimes helps is to put on an extra layer of clothing; the thought is that bodily warmth tends to slow the mind down.

BOREDOM AND OTHER CONCERNS: SOME SUGGESTIONS

Student: *What about boredom?*

LT: I asked Rinpoche about that one, too. Guess why. He said that boredom is a type of agitation, and that seen from another angle, it's simply another thought. Treat it like any thought. Touché. So in case he didn't already know it, I'd confirmed the fact that agitation is my personal favorite of the two pitfalls.

Trungpa Rinpoche, who started the huge Shambhala Sangha, said that we Westerners needed to learn to experience *lots* of boredom. I believe he felt we needed to go through and out the other side of boredom, to acceptance of even the boredom, until finally arriving at a quiet, spacious state. Remember that boredom, like amusement or stress or confusion, is in *us*, not in the situation—there's no such thing as a "boring situation," only a situation in which *we* are bored.

A common practice to help with this is to change the focus of your gaze. For example, if you've been looking at the whole figure, focus now on one particular part after another. If you've been doing that for a while, switch to the whole figure. This also keeps your eyes from getting overstrained. I've found this technique a helpful treatment for dullness, too.

Sylvia Boorstein speaks of an experience she had, with a Theravada technique of "mental noting" that helped her to keep bringing fresh awareness and presence to *each moment,* being ever present in the continual NOW, the "flow of awareness," as it's sometimes called. When she got the hang of it, she had this to say:

> A moment of mindfulness can feel ecstatic. I remember being amazed when I first began to discover the difference between talking about an experience and *being* the experience. The discovery of the rapture of mindfulness blew me away. Walking in a careful way, very present, I thought, "Talk about bizarre. *This* is bizarre: I'm totally putting my foot down." Putting a foot down is not normally the sort of thing we think of as thrilling. But it *is* thrilling. It's not the foot that is thrilling. Mindfulness is thrilling.

Student: *I've just started doing Tranquil Abiding, and I find that my mind is even MORE busy than usual! I thought this practice was about resting the mind. Mine is just roaring along. Is there something wrong with me? Am I really going to be able to do this?*

LT: This is such a common experience for people new to this practice that the ancient texts talked about it and gave it a name. As we spend time with this method, we go through successive stages of experience. The first one is referred to as a "waterfall." Now you know why! Actually our minds are very busy, with loud internal conversations all the time, but with our lens turned outward all the time, or caught up in the train of thought, we've never uncoupled ourselves from the drama and *observed* that fact before.

Congratulations! This is your first step in bringing mindfulness! I'm not kidding. It's a HUGE step, to finally really see what our minds are doing all the time. Without that step, the others can't follow. If you continue gently working with your mind as I've suggested here, that waterfall will become like a river of thoughts, then a slower one, and so on, until your mind becomes a vast, peaceful ocean. After a month or two you should notice a real difference, anyway—hopefully, even less than a month. Not bad, after countless lifetimes of the waterfall!

Student: *I don't know if this falls into the agitation category, but whenever I try to do this practice, a great sadness overwhelms me. All I do is cry. This doesn't sound like the experience we're going for, and I wonder how helpful it is for me.*

LT: Your experience is rare, but it does happen for some people. As we turn the lens from the compelling distraction of outer events, all of us sometimes experience a bubbling up of something sad, and a welling up of tears. Generally, meditation practice is the very best medicine to help us to move through and out the other side.

If this is your *consistent* experience *over time*, I would suggest not "gutting it out." In that case it tends not to get better as you go, and it could actually be detrimental for you. My suspicion is that some time spent in the right kind of psychotherapy would help. In extreme

cases where we're suffering from post-traumatic stress disorder (PTSD), I recommend body-centered PTSD techniques in addition to meditation. Some psychotherapists already include both. Body-centered trauma work such as Hakomi or Bodynamics might be the best for some people. This approach would work not so much with words, but more directly on the nervous system and body itself, to clear away this obstacle.

Once you've cleared a good chunk of that, you might try Tranquil Abiding again. Meanwhile, you could try the other practices and see how they work for you.

Dullness, the Other Pitfall

We've spoken about the pitfall of agitation; now let's explore the other common one: dullness. Rinpoche has likened those repeated moments of awareness we were talking about to a mountain stream cascading over rocks and breaking up into tiny droplets, freshening the water.

He contrasted this stream with a stagnant pond. The water is swampy because it's just sitting there. If *we* just sit there in a stupor, we're not "familiarizing" (gom) with the state we want to cultivate. As we all know, stupor is not our natural state; it's one of the Three Poisons that obscures it.

Rinpoche often tells the story of a lama and his attendant in Tibet, traveling to Lhasa, the capital. They stopped along the way, where there was a stream below, so they could make tea. The attendant, who was a practitioner, climbed down with the teapot. As he was about to fill it, he looked over his shoulder and saw a tiny cave in the rock wall. He thought, "What a *perfect* little place to meditate!" He left the teapot by the water and settled down for a good session. As happens in some cases, he fell into a deep, unconscious state much like hibernation.

Time passed and the lama started to worry. He climbed down to the water himself, saw the teapot, but no attendant. He thought some animal must have carried his attendant off and eaten him! What could he do? He continued on to Lhasa by himself and stayed for nearly a year. When it was time to come home, he took the same road. As it happened, he stopped at the same place and climbed

down to the stream with his teapot. (I guess it *was* a good stopping place.) It seems that the noise roused his attendant from his state of hibernation. The attendant called from the cave, "Are you ready for your tea?" He had no idea that a year had passed!

This is not an experience that a fellow should brag about to his friends. Rinpoche tells this story as a cautionary tale. Remaining in that blank state for a year, the young student was no closer to enlightenment, but he had lost a year of his life. Just stopping the mind is like pushing the Pause button on your DVD player. The minute you push Play again, you're right where you left off.

Many people sit in a vacuous state every day for years, thinking they're great meditators. Some of them proudly say that, even though the rest of their life is pretty miserable, while they're meditating they're feeling no pain. I feel great sadness when I think of that, and I hope they find better guidance. Really good guidance in the subtleties of mind training is all too rare.

Student: *I find myself falling asleep sometimes. What should I do?*

LT: Whenever you feel dullness, even if you're not actually falling asleep, you can lift your gaze a little bit. If you're using a visual support, gaze at the figure's forehead, shoulders, topknot, etc. I also find it really helpful to take a big breath or two, to bring in fresh oxygen and generally clean out the cobwebs. It often helps to wear thinner clothing or cool off the room a bit. There are other helpful methods, such as prostrations, which you can learn later, if you continue on this path. But for now you have a few tools in your kit.

Student: *How long should I practice?*

LT: I REALLY don't mean to be glib, but for as long as you can without your puppy-dog mind resenting it or your monkey mind hijacking it. This varies wildly, from person to person, from day to day, from year to year. If you're a beginner, I would honestly recommend starting at FIVE MINUTES. Surprising, isn't it? But remember how briefly we have a puppy do its first down-stay. Hopefully you'll give a five-minute Tranquil Abiding session your best attention. Then you can very gradually expand the number of minutes: next week, six minutes, etc.

Very soon you'll be alternating Tranquil Abiding with the next practice I'm about to introduce. Alternating the two keeps the practice fresh, alive, and focused. Your puppy-dog mind will thank you. With the two complementary practices, the session becomes more balanced and rich. The time seems to pass more quickly and easily, too.

Yet Another Pitfall: Great Experiences

If I have a great experience of bliss, clarity, or non-thought … what's not to like? Well, *maybe* nothing; it depends on what you do with it. If you take it as an encouraging sign that you're on track, and then just keep going, no problem. In the case of Shamata in particular, and meditation practice in general, we tend to have experiences of bliss, clarity, and freedom from thoughts, from time to time. These can be quite lovely—intoxicating, even. It would be quite natural to want to go back to that state again and again. That would make it a pitfall; now you're feeling desire/clinging. As we've discussed, that usually leads us more *into* Samsara, not out of it. You're trying to get the meditation to go in a very particular way. Then too, you're trying to repeat an experience from the past, so even if you could, you're preventing what you could experience *now.*

Another response would be to feel proud about your achievement, letting it drop in conversations with people, or maybe making up a story in your mind about how you'll be as a meditation teacher, now that you've come so far. As you may have guessed by now, that would be another way of going into ego identification and Samsara instead of away from it.

When you do have a positive meditation experience—called *nyam* in Tibetan—it's all right to celebrate for a moment. You just came to an encouraging signpost—good work!

Then, as with any other thought or appearance, let go of it. After all, if you're walking down a road and come to a signpost letting you know you're where you were hoping to be, do you feel all proud? Do you sit down by the post and refuse to move? You just quickly register, "Good, I'm on the right road," and continue on. If you let go of that nyam too, then you're open to all of the other experiences that you may have, further down the road … including, eventually, enlightenment.

Beginning the Session

Before you begin the session, set a planned amount of time and stick to it. If you end early, you'll quickly develop that habit and it will be VERY hard to change. This is another reason it's good to start with a relatively short time, so you'll be able to meet the plan you set for yourself. Deciding on an amount of time and actually doing the session that long gives you personal power, and lets you build momentum to do it more easily the next time. Habits, habits.

Many people set a timer. There's even a company that sells clocks that count down whatever time you set, then ring a lovely little Zen-style chime. The company is called Now and Zen. Cute. Another company, Enso, sells one called Pearl. It's more compact, which is nice, but it doesn't have a real chime. Now there are better and better alarm/alert phone apps that you could probably use as well. Just be sure your calls don't come through!

If, realistically, you have only 15 minutes, then set your time for 15, including the Clearing of the Stale Winds, dedication prayers, and so on. I did that for years, and it was easy to stick to. As I felt the benefits, I naturally wanted to make the time longer. As my mind got used to the "getting used to" (my looser translation of *gom*, the Tibetan term for meditation), I could go to 20, 30, and eventually 90 and even 120 minutes. In retreat I've done MANY sessions for 3 hours. In the beginning I never would have guessed that I'd end up being *able* to do that, much less enjoy it! Even if you never reach that length, you'll reap plenty of benefit from 20 or 30 minutes for your daily sessions. I'm not telling you this from blind faith or the exceptional experience; I'm telling you this after hearing it from dozens and dozens of students.

Ending the Session

Once you've come to the end of your session, you want to conclude it by once again remembering that you're making this effort on behalf of all beings, not just yourself. Remember: we're always trying to come from the view of the whole ocean—not just "me, the wave." So you do the other end of the "Bodhicitta bookends" that bracket your session.

Because all beings are also stuck in this predicament called *Samsara*, we want to end with prayers for their eventual freedom, along with our own—once again, the Two Purposes. I've included some traditional Tibetan prayers for you to say at that point. I've offered them in both English, because of course you need the meaning, and Tibetan, because some of you might want to use the same sounds that many others have used for so many years. The sounds themselves do carry power, and that's worth something

too. The chanted Tibetan has a rhythm to it which is sweet and compelling. If you ever find yourself with Tibetans, they'll most likely know one or two of these prayers, so you'll be able to "sing along." Then too, I've noticed that some Westerners just get a kick out of Tibetan clothes, sounds, prayer flags, and so on. So for all those reasons I thought I'd include the Tibetan too.

This first prayer is for Ngöndro, the set of Preliminary Practices. Despite the name, you would actually do these practices after already making some progress with the ones in this book (but you can do the prayer anytime). There is a dedication/aspirational prayer at the end of the session, which kind of says it all, in my mind. But an added benefit is that if you decide to do the Preliminary Practices, you'll already know the ending prayer. Here it is, along with another one:

DEDICATION OF MERIT

Gewa di yi nyur du dak   Orgyen Lama drup gyur ne
By this virtue may I swiftly   *Attain the state of the Lama of Orgyen,*[*]

Drowa jik kyang ma lü pa   De yi sa la gö par shog
And bring all beings without exception   *To that level.*

or:

By the power of this compassionate practice,
May suffering be transformed into peace.
May the hearts of all beings be open,   *Now that's real freedom!*
And their wisdom radiate from within.[**]

If you already have a Root Lama, you would conclude with his or her long-life prayer.

In Conclusion

So take your meditation a moment at a time. Each time you actually realize you're following after thoughts, *rejoice* at your realization … and drop back into resting your eyes on the image, and resting your mind in fresh, alive, joyful awareness. And that next moment of pure Tranquil Abiding will pass too, but that's okay. You'll have another fresh one. Many per session, I hope!

Over time, I became able to take a vacation in the middle of daily life, in just the same way as I do in those moments of awareness. "Oh, I don't have to follow that." *Now that's real freedom!*

---

[*]   One of many epithets for Guru Rinpoche, who of course reached full enlightenment.
[**] Used by the Tergar Sangha, led by Mingyur Rinpoche.

I'll say it again: *That's real freedom.* Having to follow after your thoughts like a dog on a leash isn't. It's slavery, just like my having to buy and smoke cigarettes was also slavery. When our mind plays a painful scene over and over, sometimes we can't seem to stop it. But replaying it is like picking at a wound so that it can never heal. If someone hits you with a tennis racket, that person did it once and moved on. But if you play the scene over and over again, it's like you've picked up the racket and continued the beating. You've just beaten yourself a hundred times. Yet we can't always stop ourselves through force of will. Therefore, training is needed.

Not only was it a relief to be freer of such things, but it kept me from compulsively following a neurosis-driven train of thought that would have led to unfortunate speech and/or action, planting karmic seeds, sending me on another turn of the wheel. Needless to say, it wouldn't have helped the other person involved, either. How many of us have *known* we should leave a situation or a nasty remark well enough alone … and *can't?* Of course, I still find myself wishing I'd left well enough alone many times on any and all of the above. Practice, practice.

FURTHER STUDY

I've given you a very quick introduction to Tranquil Abiding, or Shamata. If you find you really want to do this practice regularly, there are many sources that go into it much more fully. The best two I know of are very different and complement each other well.

The first is a meditation kit by Joseph Goldstein and Sharon Salzberg. They studied this method with great masters in Burma and Thailand for years, then studied, practiced, and taught it in America for decades. They're genuine masters in their own right, and make it all very accessible—a winning combination! You can buy their kit at Sounds True or at many Dharma bookstores. Ours, for example.

My one caveat is that their version of this method was learned from the Theravada Lineage, so it differs in some ways from the particular version I've just laid out for you. For example, they don't specify to breathe through the mouth, but in my particular lineage, we do. They insist that you remain motionless during the sitting portion (they alternate this practice with Walking Meditation); we don't. There are other differences too. If you take one of their retreats, you're free to decide what variations you want to do, except that of course if they specify something like Walking Meditation, you'll probably want to go with the program. But they won't object if you keep your eyes open, for example.

Another difference with the Insight Meditation Society, where Goldstein and Salzberg teach, is that though they begin with Shamata, they very quickly introduce Vipassana, or Insight Meditation, which is a partner to Shamata. In Rinpoche's style of teaching, he brings in other practices before Vipassana, and generally doesn't emphasize either Shamata or Vipassana nearly as much. Unlike the Insight Meditation Society, he doesn't see them as an end in themselves.

The Shamata I've taught here is designed to prepare you for a succession of Vajrayana practices. If you intend to go on to other Vajrayana practices—particularly the ones in our lineage—you'll naturally want to do Tranquil Abiding more like the variation in this book, and work in the other practices rather than going immediately to Vipassana and emphasizing it.

I also strongly recommend a book on this topic by my lama, Tulku Sangak Rinpoche. It will be available at Namchak.org as soon as it's published—check the website for details. It's a nice balance to the book you're now reading as well as the kit I just mentioned, in that it gives lots of background and instruction that I don't include here. I've given you a bit of introduction and context that I think is essential for Westerners, because that's what I can do as a Westerner. And unlike the Insight Meditation Society folks, I'm a Vajrayana (Tibetan Buddhist) practitioner.

Rinpoche is Tibetan, and, though he doesn't even speak English (of course he had the book translated), his book will give you further context in a very different way, and bring you a level of depth and understanding—both intellectually and experientially—that only he can offer.

One other master who is both a Westerner and a Vajrayana teacher is Pema Chödrön. You can find books and recordings of her teaching Shamata.

If you really want to check into this practice, you'll make it easier for yourself if you just *go do* a Shamata retreat. Nothing can replace having live teachings from a qualified teacher, and then having the optimal container—retreat—in which to road-test the teachings.

One teacher, Anam Thubten Rinpoche, who does this quite well is Tibetan, but his English is better than many Americans'. He especially enjoys using colloquial turns of phrase, to the delight of his listeners. He really gets the point across, too.

Ewam and Namchak are two 501(c)(3) charters under our one Sangha, led by Tulku Sangak Rinpoche. If you would like to try one of our Shamata retreats, you can look at our schedule at www.namchak.org. The website for Ewam International is www.ewam.org

Instructional audio for this practice is available at www.namchak.org

SCIENCE TIDBIT

My Own Little Experiment

A few years ago, I had the chance to use a biofeedback device that measured the coordination or "coherence" (as HeartMath, the creators of the device called it) between my brain and my heart. (For a fuller explanation, check www.heartmath.org.) Normally it takes training to coordinate them much at all. When we have negative emotions, the line on the readout graph looks squiggly, random, and, well, incoherent. When there's 100% coherence, it shows a perfect sine wave—perfectly round hills and valleys.

When I was first hooked up to the device, the graph readout showed a sloppy sine wave. There were hills and valleys, but rough. Then the coach asked me to imagine a bear chasing me. At the moment I clearly visualized and felt the experience in my mind, the biofeedback readout suddenly went completely haphazard. It looked like the track of an insane bug.

Then he asked me to think of something inspiring.

I immediately knew what to choose: my favorite part of my meditation sessions—why not? In that part, my Root Lama, Rinpoche, appears as Guru Rinpoche, the enlightened master who transformed Tibet into a Buddhist country. The image is colorful, beautiful, and inspiring. And for me it's enlivened by my feeling the presence of my own master, Rinpoche. I closed my eyes and recited the beautiful little prayer that goes with it, imagining Rinpoche slowly coming down into my heart. Then we mingled together into one awareness. I rested there.

When I opened my eyes, the readout showed a perfect sine wave. The biofeedback technician was shocked. Normally, after working with the device for weeks, people can get a reasonably coherent sine wave, indicating coherence between the brain and heart. I had immediately gone to 100% coherence and stayed there the entire time. Of course, as soon as I stopped the visualization, the readout showed a sloppy sine wave like the one in the beginning. I still needed to do more practice!

When I tried this again later, with other Buddhist practices, I had exactly the same results. When I opened my eyes I was jubilant, saying, "Hey, this shit works!" (Whereupon, the sine wave immediately got sloppy again.) But since I'd already experienced my own inner transformation and gotten feedback from many other people, why was I surprised? Why did I need a machine to validate what I already knew? Still, for some reason I thought you might like to hear about this.

TONGLEN

Tranquil Abiding helps us calm the waters of the mind, allowing us to experience truth more clearly. We can learn a lot through studying the nature of the mind and reality, but we can't stop there.

Tranquil Abiding helps us to *see* for *ourselves*, through stilling the mind and experiencing insight. Through connecting with *others*, as a compassionate act, *Tonglen* helps us *feel* how we're not separate from the rest of the ocean.

This balance is important. The Tibetan scriptures speak of many pairs. I've already mentioned their definition of enlightenment: cleansing our obscurations (the windshield) and fully maturing our buddha qualities (evidence of our *Buddha Nature*.) Tranquil Abiding helps with the former; Tonglen with the latter. Another pair is wisdom (Tranquil Abiding) and compassion (Tonglen).

I've said that Vajrayana (Tibetan Buddhism) meets us where we are, and supports us in our journey from there. So it is with Tonglen. From time to time, we will all imagine someone and have an imagined interaction with them. Well, here, you get to do that as an official part of the exercise! We also tend to feel great compassion for those we're close to in our lives, and not so much for others. We get to start with that tendency, then expand from there.

I'll get to the specifics in a bit, but first I want to tell you a little more about Tonglen in general. As you progress along this path, you'll see that we're often given methods that alternate between purifying our karmic windshield and expanding our buddha qualities—again, the Tibetan understanding of cleansing away impurities and maturing our Buddha Nature, sangye. As Rinpoche has said, wisdom without compassion can lead to the creation of atom bombs. Compassion without wisdom is ineffectual, and can just be a nice sentiment. We don't want to develop one while ignoring the other. Now that you've started cleaning your windshield, here's a practice that expands your capacity for compassion.

Tonglen is a Tibetan form of compassion practice that's used in different forms in all of the lineages of the Dharma. Within Vajrayana (Tibetan Buddhism) there are many sub-branch lineages, all of which practice Tonglen, but as with many of the practices, they vary a bit, from one to another. The word *Tonglen* means "sending and receiving" in Tibetan. In this practice, we basically imagine breathing in the suffering of others and breathing out our wish for them to be happy.

The Setup

Before beginning the practice, I often bring to mind some kind of suffering I'm experiencing in my own life at the moment. Since my life is rarely perfect, I can usually find a juicy subject for my practice. Sometimes I've heard of another person who's suffering terribly, so I naturally focus on that. Then too, if I hear of a natural disaster or war that destroyed many lives, it's natural for me to focus on those people and animals. Wherever my passion is, that's a likely place for me to start the practice of *com*passion.

For the moment, let's say you've picked your own suffering. Let's say it's the feeling that your life is meaningless, and, naturally, you're upset about that. You've got a job that's meaningless; when you go home, there's not much meaning going on. You feel powerless to change your life, and you're coming ever closer to the end of it without hope of doing more meaningful work or having more meaningful relationships. I believe this is what Thoreau was referring to when he spoke of most people leading lives of "quiet desperation." In this situation, you may start with doing Tonglen for yourself, or you may take that strong feeling and begin practicing for someone you care about who is enduring a similar kind of suffering: a dearth of meaning in their life.

If another kind of suffering (yours or someone else's) is more immediate, though, such as loneliness, grief, guilt, or frustration, then go ahead and pick that. In other words, choose whatever feels most acute and important to you as you prepare to begin.

Tibetans traditionally begin by imagining someone they feel natural sympathy for, who has a particular kind of suffering. Many of us in the West have found it really helpful to start with ourselves, an approach which may sound narrowly egotistical, but isn't necessarily. Since most of us haven't got enough compassion for *ourselves,* what basis do we have for expanding that toward others? The Golden Rule, "Do unto others as you would have them do unto you," doesn't work if we don't have compassion for ourselves. It's the same with "Love thy neighbor as thyself." Because we Westerners tend to *think about* painful circumstances (our own, or others') rather than fully and feelingly experience them, we often do Tonglen more as an intellectual exercise than as a (com)passionate act. This practice is intended to strongly engage our emotion— the *positive* emotion of compassion.

So the two decisions to make before you start are: (1) which "theme" you're working with and (2) whether you'll start with yourself or another.

✸ *The Actual Practice*

AS YOU BEGIN

Sit with your back relatively straight, so your yeshe winds are likely to be stronger. The Tibetans say, "When the spine is straight, the channels are straight. When the channels are straight, the winds go straight. When the winds go straight, the mind goes straight." After

having done the Tibetan Nose Blow, you are no doubt coming to understand how this works.

Bring to mind the subject of suffering you've chosen. Again, I recommend that you generally start the session by doing Tonglen for yourself. You then go the next rung out: sending and receiving for someone else—someone you easily feel strong compassion for—who is experiencing the same kind of suffering you have in your life right now. For example, if I'm suffering from my own grief, and I bring to mind a Tibetan friend I know whose father and brothers were all suddenly taken away and never heard from again, I can REALLY feel for her.

MAIN PART

As you begin this practice, I'm assuming you've just finished doing Shamata, but if not, first flash on that ultimate ocean of awareness. It has many qualities—such as vastness, absolute power (to create everything), and absolute compassion. This Absolute, or Ultimate, Bodhicitta comes from the awakened mind of Absolute Truth. So "change channels," and bring your mind to that Absolute Bodhicitta level for just a moment, as a starting point for this practice.

Now, clearly imagine someone in front of you, someone you easily feel sympathetic to—as we discussed, it could be yourself. Even if the eventual focus of your practice is someone else, I highly recommend you *precede* this by imagining yourself, in your own suffering. Place your small, suffering self in your heart, or out in front—experiment with what works best for you. Only then should you proceed to do Tonglen, first for yourself, then for your suffering friend, etc., in ever-widening circles. If you've chosen victims of a natural disaster or war or catastrophe, then go ahead and start with them. I'd recommend imagining them as individuals, one by one, to start with, so it's more immediate and intimate. See each face in pain.

Perhaps you've already brought your own loneliness up and are feeling the pain of that. Now you open yourself up to the pain of your friend. Now you're *really* feeling compassion! Of *course* you want to take away their suffering. Now's your chance!

In this movie you're doing, you breathe in their suffering in the form of dark clouds, coming from them right into your heart. Yes, you breathe it into your heart, where you feel your compassion for them, the part that passionately doesn't want them to suffer, the part that wants to take their suffering away. This is com*passion* at work. At this point, I quite often have tears.

In this next part of your movie (sometimes it's *good* to make movies in your mind!), you breathe out your wish for them to be happy. This wish appears as white, sparkling clouds, going from your heart to them. It surrounds and soaks into them.

If they're suffering from a useless life, now you imagine them doing what they'd REALLY love to do, something that fills their hearts with satisfaction. They're smiling.

If the suffering is loneliness, we imagine them basking in love. Their face is transformed into a huge smile. They're glowing. We find ourselves smiling too. We want them to be *completely* free from suffering and happy *always*.

Let yourself really *feel* all this. By now, I often find that my eyes still have tears and my mouth now has a smile.

Breathe in the suffering again. You probably didn't take it all away in the first breath, and you don't want to leave any suffering, or skimp on giving them joy. You want them *100%, permanently happy!* Why not eternal bliss?! Send out the joy to them again, on the sparkling clouds of your breath, imagining that now they're completely enlightened, and will remain eternally joyful.

As you do this a few times you, too, might notice tears in your eyes and a smile on your face, all at the same time. It's not required, but it sometimes happens that way. We feel the suffering as we breathe in, AND we feel satisfaction and joy as we *finally* have a chance to *do* something about it.

But let's not stop there. That's only one person. Now do the same operation for someone else whom you can easily feel compassion for, who has (or has had) a similar kind of suffering. Do a few breaths for them. Now another, then another. People—maybe animals too—are starting to pop up all around you.

Now you're ready to move to the next rung out. In this rung of concentric circles, you imagine people (or creatures) you don't have such strong affinity for, perhaps distant acquaintances or people you've heard about in passing. Maybe they have a similar kind of suffering too. Now that we've gotten a tide of compassion going in ourselves, we can feel just about as passionate about ridding them of suffering too. Now that we think of it, we want *them* to be happy too. Ultimate, everlasting joy—sure! So we breathe for them.

For the next rung out, imagine whole *classes* of creatures: waifs on the streets of Mexico City, slaves, drug addicts, bullied kids, people dying of cancer, whatever goes with your theme. Riding on the strong waves of passionate compassion, we strongly want to take away their misery too, and make them happy. We breathe for them.

After you've done this practice for a few weeks, you may want to really stretch your compassion muscles and do Tonglen for somebody you don't like, someone who's caused you trouble. They might even be a troublemaker or enemy. At this point in the practice, you might be able to see them simply as a misguided sentient being, trying to pursue happiness and ending up with suffering. (Sound like anybody you know? Everybody? Yourself, even?) Breathe for them.

At some time or another, EVERY being in Samsara, both seen and unseen, has certainly suffered similarly. They will in the future, too. Since linear time is another illusory appearance, we can breathe for ALL of them. That means absolutely everybody. Who would we want to leave out? So, last, breathe for them all.

Now rest for a bit. This is often a good time to do Shamata again.

DEDICATION AND ASPIRATIONS

Finish with the concluding prayers. Then pause for a moment before rushing back into the fray of daily life. You've earned that moment of basking—why not take it?

❀ Questions (and Answers!)

Student: *I'm a little nervous: if I do Tonglen for someone with cancer, will I get cancer?*

LT: I must confess I had the same worry too, in the beginning. Only if you're a very highly realized being could that happen, in which case you'd also be able to transform their affliction. In either case, then, I don't see how you'd get sick. Let me use a really easy example: If you did Tonglen for someone with a broken arm, would your arm break? If you did Tonglen for someone whose beloved dog had died, would yours suddenly die? You see my point?

Student: *Well, when you put it like that …*

Student: *I find I'm skittish about breathing in someone's problems. I really don't want to let that in. To be honest, I'm actually scared of the feeling.*

LT: This brings us to a very important distinction: You're not breathing in their *story*. You're breathing in their *suffering*. Remember, too, that those dark clouds get transformed to bright ones with every breath. How? The next very important point: *through your strong feeling of compassion*. The transformation happens through the power of the desire in our heart for that person to be free of suffering and to be happy. It's kind of like photosynthesis: a plant "breathes" in carbon dioxide and "breathes" out oxygen; in Tonglen, we breathe in suffering and breathe out happiness.

The stronger your feeling of compassion, the less you have to worry about getting brought down by the dark cloud.

To put it another way, you won't get weighed down by the dark clouds of suffering if you want them to be happy. Why? Since your very feeling of compassion wants to take away their suffering and make them happy, the visualization will naturally follow your mind, your intention, what you want to happen. The compassion is the catalyst.

Here's a key point: Remember to keep your breaths of equal length and intensity. Paltry breaths in, with big, strong breaths out, is anemic compassion. Then again, if you do intense in-breaths, really taking in the suffering, then puny out-breaths, you'll end up feeling depleted and depressed. So keep your breaths long, equal, and full, allowing your robust feelings of compassion to perform the alchemy.

Student: *What if I come upon a car accident or I'm visiting a relative in the hospital? Can I do Tonglen right then and there?*

LT: Triage Tonglen is an excellent thing to do! We're inspired in the moment, and there seems to be some scientific proof that prayer really may help with healing, for example. Why leave it only for the meditation room? That doesn't mean we should give up doing the full practice as I've described, but in-the-moment Tonglen for someone suffering right in front of you is a great thing to do in addition. Besides, it could have a very real effect.

Student: *I tried doing it for my husband, who I'm planning to divorce. When it came to the in-breath, I just really didn't want to take anything in. The same thing happened when I tried it with George Bush. What should I do?*

LT: George Bush? Your almost-ex-husband? You're really going for extra credit! Seriously, you could do one of two things: (1) Remember that you're only taking in his *suffering*, not his personality, his politics, his bad vibes, or whatever it is that you really don't want to take in. As I mentioned before, you're seeing him as a misguided sentient being with suffering, and then breathing in the suffering itself. If you think of the karma that George or whoever is gathering for themselves, you can then imagine their next life and feel compassion. (2) You can just opt out of doing Tonglen for him at this point. There's no law that says you have to do Tonglen for him today—this year, even.

Many Tibetans were eventually able to have great, sincere compassion for the Chinese, even their torturers. When one monk who had been tortured and beaten countless times in his thirty-five years in prison was finally released and arrived in India, he had an audience with His Holiness the Dalai Lama. The Dalai Lama asked him what his greatest fear was during that whole, harrowing time. "My greatest fear was that I might lose compassion," he replied. But then he said that when he saw the great unhappiness in his torturer's face, he found himself able to feel compassion for him. His fear was laid to rest.

Student: *I'm embarrassed to say that I find my mind wandering off track from time to time.*

LT: Yeah, so does mine. You noticed that with Shamata, too, no doubt. Here's a little secret I'll let you in on: EVERY practice, on one level, is about forgetting and remembering, forgetting and remembering. Slowly, slowly, we make progress. The point is that we're trying to be more mindful. We're not there yet, which is why we call all of these "practice." Please practice compassion for your wiggly-puppy mind. Practice compassion for yourself.

🌼 *Additional Comments*

Whenever I've been suffering from physical or mental pain, I almost always find that my lens has gotten very small. The pain fills the whole lens. This is just what I don't want, because then my experience is 100% suffering. How ironic. How human. This practice opens the lens *w i d e*. The pain is exactly the same, but it takes up a tiny fraction of my lens now. Even though this practice hasn't fixed my actual problem, it transforms the experience altogether. That's worth a lot!

Beyond that, the more we do this practice, the more we expand our capacity for compassion. You don't have to take my word. Many *f*MRI studies done at the University of Wisconsin–Madison, and elsewhere have consistently measured levels of brain activity, some in particular locations, and some at particular wave frequencies, that indicate high levels of compassion in longtime Buddhist meditators. We're talking, literally off the charts! This was particularly true while they were meditating, but even in between sessions.

For more specifics on this, you could start by reading Chapter 16 of *Happiness*, by Matthieu Ricard, or by visiting the website of the Mind & Life Institute. In addition to the studies, the Institute lists books they've generated from the meetings they've held between scientists and the Dalai Lama. You might find a number of them interesting. Frankly, I find I'm like a kid in a candy store when I look at their book list!

As you may have guessed, Tonglen is a powerful practice, if done full-heartedly. It can be very healing. It can also be very challenging. Again, practice compassion on yourself, so you can be successful with this. Only you can judge how long your sessions should be. While you're still new to the practice, I'd recommend doing it for five minutes at a time, alternating it with Shamata. And, as with Shamata, you can lengthen your sessions as you become more familiar with the practice.

RECOMMENDED READING

There's one book on this topic that I'd recommend—I'd say it's required reading if you're serious about doing Tonglen. It's a tiny little book, devoted entirely to this practice, titled *Tonglen, the Path of Transformation* (hope you can remember that title). The author is a nun in the Tibetan tradition, and an American by birth, Pema Chödrön. Her instructions are very similar to what we've covered, but she goes into some more areas there than I do here. Pema Chödrön's style is very human, direct, laser-like, yet utterly compassionate. She's offered many excellent books and recordings on Buddhist topics, and I've really appreciated every one of them I've experienced. You can find her offerings at Sounds True and Shambhala Publishing.

Instructional audio for this practice is available at www.namchak.org

DOING DAILY PRACTICE

 *Round Robin*

I've thrown a lot at you, and when you sit down to practice, you might be just a wee bit confused. What do you do first? Then what? For how long? I've found for myself that the part of my mind that's doing practice is not the part that can go down a list. Besides, after the intensity of doing some Tonglen, for example, it's hard to remember where I'm at in the whole, larger progression of the session. So later in this chapter I've provided you with a simple list you can look through right now. And I've created a separate card you can keep by your meditation spot. Then again, you could just bookmark that page. You can also write out a shorter version, once you're really used to it.

With our busy modern lives, I find that it's difficult to stick with one form of meditation for a long time. Besides, as you remember, Rinpoche recommends breaking up the sessions to keep our experience fresh, while at the same time keeping us on the cushion. Chagdüd Tulku also recommends alternating practices for short periods, and I've found this really effective, especially for beginners.

One Tibetan doctor noticed that many of the students at our center, like most of his Western patients, had too much of the air element (similar to the old Western medical model of the "humors"). He told all of them not to meditate consecutively for more than *five minutes,* because the restless air element couldn't handle it and they would only get more agitated. To address the problem, I recommended this Round Robin Meditation method of alternating practices every five minutes. Everyone who tried it found they could sit for twenty minutes without the ill effects the doctor had warned them about.

Since I've found most Americans respond well to this round robin method, I tend to think the doctor is onto something. I also like that the round robin has us changing gears all the time, keeping our practice fresh. Here, then, is a suggested procession of events for your sessions, which you can modify in some ways as you go. I've put it on the next page.

✸ *Sample Daily Practice Session*

ROUND ROBIN MEDITATION

✺ 1 minute or less: Check motivation for doing this practice, in this session. Bring forward Bodhicitta motivation (the Two Purposes) if necessary. (Hint: It almost always needs a little bringing forward, but don't expect it to be 100% before moving on—that's what the practice is *for*, after all.)

✺ 10 to 15 seconds: Offer three short prostrations. *Optional.* (Description on pages 213 to 214.)

✺ 1 minute: Clearing the Stale Winds. Rest.

✺ 5 minutes: Shamata.

✺ 5 minutes: Tonglen.

✺ 5 minutes: Shamata.

(*Optional:* If you have the time, you could alternate between Shamata and Tonglen again and again. It's good to end this part with at least a bit of Shamata, before going to the concluding stage.)

✺ 30 seconds: Dedication of merit and aspirational prayers.

If you have a Root Lama, you would recite their long-life prayer at this time.

Instructional audio for this practice is available at www.namchak.org

 The Practice of Doing Daily Practice

The easiest part about daily practice is actually doing it. In my years of practicing and teaching, I've seen that the hardest thing is *getting one's butt to the cushion on a daily basis.* In other words, *starting* is the hardest part. But of course, without starting, there's no practice at all. So here are some tips to help you with what is, for many, the most difficult practice: The Doing of Daily Practice.

First of all, I suggest that in the beginning you give yourself a really attainable goal: fifteen minutes a day. Trust me: Thirty minutes every other day won't work as well. For one thing, every other day is a much harder rhythm to establish than every day. For another, we want to be compassionate with our minds and not make them try to do something so new for more than fifteen minutes a day, in the beginning. And a third reason: When learning a new language, it won't work to do two hours on Saturday, and nothing the rest of the week. It's much better to do a little every day. The same is true for learning a musical instrument. This training is no different. And our minds, like our muscles, seem to "learn" to do more effectively what we do more regularly.

Yet another reason for starting with fifteen-minute sessions is that it's hard to come up with a believable excuse for not taking *fifteen minutes.* When we tell ourselves that we don't *have* time for something, it almost always means that we're choosing not to *take* time for something (fifteen minutes a day still leaves you twenty-three hours and forty-five minutes for other pursuits—and if your life's so hectic that you don't feel as though you can spare fifteen minutes, you really *do* need some Tranquil Abiding).

The last reason is that our whole purpose here is to change long-established habits of the mind. It's been proven that doing something daily is most effective at changing habits. The rule that I keep hearing again and again is that if you do something every day for twenty-one days, it becomes a habit. Alcoholics Anonymous uses this theory in their work.

I should probably repeat my personal favorite: I think of my daily practice as a vacation. We all need a vacation, but even when we take a trip to Hawaii, we take our busy minds with us. Doing practice can feel even better than sitting on a beach, stewing about the nasty thing so-and-so said to you. This is a REAL vacation, and I want to take it every day!

This is a REAL vacation, and I want to take it every day!

Okay, I have to confess that I hardly ever take an actual vacation, in the normal sense of the word. I'm kind of a workaholic (perhaps the apple doesn't fall far from the paternal tree?). So the motivator that usually actually gets me on the cushion is to say, "Since this will help all of your work go better, this is your most important work for the day." I once saw a refrigerator magnet that said something like, "When I don't meditate, I waste a lot more time running around like a chicken with its head cut off." The five years I didn't meditate proved these last two points to me, about efficiency and focus, beyond a doubt.

Working It into Your Schedule

This is a key to success in your practice, so let's spend some time on this one. It's best, but not essential, to do your sessions just as you wake up in the morning. Most Tibetan practitioners do theirs at this time because the border between sleeping and waking is an especially good opportunity to catch the mind at the beginning of the day, before it's fallen into its old ruts and gained momentum. We step into the day with a bit more mindfulness, and all the thousands of decisions that you make that day can be made from that state of mind. Then too, early morning is usually a much quieter time, with a calm, clear feeling to it—none of the bustle of the rest of the day. The waters of the mind tend to be more settled, clear, and fresh … especially after Clearing the Stale Winds!

When I had small children at home, they were early risers, so I had trouble getting a good session in before they woke up. Tibetans often get up at incredibly early hours, to make time for their sessions. Being a lazy American who needs something like a full night's sleep, I did the next best thing and meditated at night after the kids were asleep, and hopefully *before* I was (when I was on the *other* border between sleeping and waking).

Whatever time you've decided on, a key to success is *keeping to your sessions in the same part of your daily schedule.* I think that's why we succeed in brushing our teeth so regularly: the momentum of routine and habit is unbelievably strong. We've talked about how negative momentum can work against us, but we can use positive momentum to work in our favor, once the good habit is

established. If your bedtime varies, that's less than optimal but still workable. Just as you can brush your teeth a bit later because you're going to bed a bit later, you can meditate a bit later too. If you can't do your session at exactly the same time each day, just keep it in the same part of your routine.

If you're doing your sessions at some place or time other than sitting up in bed first thing in the morning, begin by facing your shrine, or at least a picture of a buddha and/or your Root Lama. If you're going to offer three prostrations, this is when you would do them.

How to Do a Prostration

Before I describe *how*, I should probably mention to *whom/what* we prostrate. We prostrate to the Three Jewels: (1) the enlightened mind of the Buddha, (2) his teachings—the Dharma—which instruct us how to become enlightened ourselves, and (3) the Sangha, the congregation of like-minded people pursuing this path of enlightenment.

The Buddha saw all three of these as essential if we're to reach our goal of enlightenment. I'll say more about this a bit later. For now I'll say that, in addition to daily practice, it's a wonderful support to have others—Sangha—reading, studying, and practicing this same material with you. If you don't already have such friends at hand, please look at Appendix A for how you can find like-minded people nearby, and how to set up a weekly study/practice group. Or you can find it all on our website: namchak.org.

To put it *very* succinctly, prostrations are yet another way to loosen our ferocious grip on ego identification: lower mind bows to higher mind; small self to the larger Self.

We bow down on the floor. We literally get down on our knees and lower our heads to the ground. In a full prostration, we then stretch out, face down. Then reverse the whole process to get up. Before and after each sequence, we put our hands together in prayer position, then touch the forehead, throat, and heart. When we do that at the end of one prostration, it serves as the beginning of the next.

I experience prostration as a kinesthetic reminder that, in right relationship, the lower self serves the greater Self. This action gets that thought literally *into our bones*. We touch the three places and bow down, paying homage to the greater Self with our body, speech, and mind. If you have a Root Lama, they hopefully have that meaning for you, so you offer the prostrations to them. In any case, you can use the picture of an enlightened being, such as the one included in this packet. Both the lama and the enlightened being represent the Three Jewels in this way: their body is the Sangha, their speech is the Dharma, and their mind is the Buddha. Now that you've reminded yourself in such a dramatic way of right relationship of self to Self, you're ready to begin your session.

Place

As with other regular routines, we can really be supported by having a regular *place* to practice, with conditions that work in our favor.

So you'll need a place that's conducive to practice. As with practicing the piano, you don't go out and perform before you've practiced at home, with no pressure or distractions. So it is with this kind of practice. The practices are designed to help you eventually apply your developing capacities in daily life, but we can hardly expect ourselves to do that right away. I wouldn't suggest performing a concert after your first piano lesson either.

Being isolated from outside demands will clearly help. I knew one practitioner who answered his phone while in "session"! His progress was disappointing, of course. So don't just turn your cell phone off—turn it off and put it in another room. The whole point is to give ourselves the chance not to respond to stimuli and distractions from the outside for a bit. Then we can turn the lens inward.

Another support I've already mentioned is a statue or picture of an enlightened being. Tibetans like to have statues and paintings of enlightened deities and great masters where they practice. They also keep relics there. Scientists have now confirmed that states of mind can be infectious. Tibetans already knew this, as well as the power of archetypal images. We might as well have that knowledge work for us.

If you create a special place or shrine that's just for meditation, that can really work well for you. Our brains work by association, and if we associate that place with meditation, we'll have even more momentum working for us. Time and again, students have reported their practice improving by leaps and bounds as soon as they set up a meditation spot for themselves.

✤ *Frame of Mind*

If I gave you one piece of advice, from one Western practitioner to another, it would be this: Practice compassion for *your own mind* as you train it. As I've said, if you start to train a puppy and immediately expect it to do tricks, do a "down-stay" for an hour, or some other such demand, you're going to have a neurotic puppy that absolutely hates training sessions. It will be a fighting match all the way. Given the power of the human unconscious mind, I guarantee that if you take such a Nazi approach to practice, you'll make no progress and you'll eventually give up practice altogether.

Remember, it's taken you lifetimes to get to this opportunity. Moving forward five minutes at a time now is still more progress than you've made in, literally, ages.

The good news is that, if you don't push yourself unrealistically, practice sessions can feel good. Really good.

Something the Tibetans call the Four Thoughts also puts us into the proper frame of mind. It actually *uses* our natural tendency to think about things. It brings even that onto the path, and we emerge from these four contemplations having a much clearer, broader, and deeper understanding of our place in the great scheme of things. This helps not only with practice but with life. I want to remind you of the woman whose sister had suddenly died. She said that it was mostly having contemplated the Four Thoughts that had served her so well in her grief. Without having expanded her worldview and brought it into focus, she would have handled her sister's death badly. None of us knows when something tragic like that will happen to us. We can only know that eventually something will happen. Such is life.

> "*Meditation is really just learning to enjoy your experience, so you don't have to tense up. Don't make meditation a project like everything else.*"
>
> —ELIZABETH MATTIS-NAMGYEL

Even when nothing terrible is happening, to have consciously and thoroughly worked out your worldview is a satisfying thing. We haven't had much opportunity or guidance in the past, so here's an opportunity to really dive into it.

In Closing: Some Words of Advice

Now that you've taken in a *feast* of new information, it's time to digest. Please take your time with the vast wealth of knowledge and skillful means that you've just perused. Again, study, contemplate, revisit, and practice it all—doing the Round Robin Meditation, or doing full sessions on whatever you're working on, if that works better for you. Take to heart whichever concepts ring true (and keep an open mind and heart for those that still seem to be a stretch).

After you've drunk deeply of these ideas and practices for a few months, you'll have just *begun* to taste the benefits. Trust me on this one. Better yet, *don't* trust me. Keep on with these practices and see for yourself!

It doesn't matter how smart or how spiritual you are—charging ahead will be of little benefit. In fact, the more seriously you want to pursue this, the more you'll get out of these thoughts and methods by going bit by bit, sinking deeply into each part.

During the course of your day, try out some understanding you've achieved in meditation. Or, going the other way, as you witness or experience events, or interact with others, see if any of your recent understandings shed light on these moments. The illumination could come from your Tonglen practice, from the Four Thoughts, from Shamata.

There are many, many fine nuggets of understanding to be found, one by one, as you read, contemplate, and practice. With these nuggets you can build a worldview that's fully considered, tested, and made your own. Why rush?

If you build a hasty foundation, your house won't be straight or stand very long.

From another point of view, I hope you're enjoying the *doing* of these contemplations and practices, enjoying the adventure of inquiry. I hope you're finding meaning in the ideas you've encountered, and I sincerely hope you study further from other books and especially real, live teachers. This book was never intended to give you all of even the foundational understandings.

A Word or Two About Drugs

I'm speaking of the "recreational" kind. Often, while you're on whatever it is, you think you're seeing the world more clearly. Sometimes you may indeed get a glimpse of something—sort of like walking in the middle of the forest, and then climbing a tree. Maybe we can see much farther, but, even then, we still have to climb down and keep walking if we're ever going to get "home."

In most cases, though, if we think we're brilliant when we write that poem while high, we read it in the morning and it's incomprehensible or embarrassing—or both. While we were drunk, other people—who weren't—saw us not as clever and charming but as slobbery and obnoxious.

One fellow, who had been meditating for years and was very fond of his dope, had this to say: "Meditating, then getting high, is like washing your white pants, putting them on, and then sitting in the mud." Another indulger of similar habits confessed that getting drunk or high was like putting a paper bag over his head. Perhaps not an effective enlightenment technique.

If you honestly want to give the things in this book a real try, you won't even know what they can do for you, much less actually derive a whole lot of benefit, if you cause more mental obscuration with drugs. Our windshields are already smeared with Samsaric gunk—we don't need to slather on another layer of drug sludge. It's simply the opposite direction from the one you're trying to pursue.

But let's face it: We all, in one form or another, take refuge in some form of addiction, and it's very hard to stop. This is a kind of catch-22 again. As with the greater catch-22 I talked about, you can work slowly and consistently with your mind on this. As in my case with cigarettes, I'm hoping that, as you do practice, you get *enough* benefit that you can begin to take refuge in the experiences you're having in practice instead of your addiction of choice. Probably the thing I felt most immediately happy about, once I no longer smoked, was that I was no longer a slave to it. I was free.

In addressing your addictions, you can, of course, complement your practice with other resources. Support groups such as Alcoholics Anonymous, and other programs with similar approaches, have helped many free themselves from addiction. Their tenets can dovetail quite nicely with the worldview and methods presented here.

As I've mentioned, my worst addiction when I started Buddhist practice was smoking. I couldn't stop, even though I was terrified of cancer. Nicotine is a kind of speed, and it's more addictive than heroin. If you decide to quit smoking you might find that a nicotine patch helps you during the first week or so.

And for other addictions or self-destructive patterns, you can seek out alternatives, methods, and support to help you get unstuck and moving forward.

If you already have something larger you can go to for refuge—something beyond the vicissitudes of everyday, problematic life and death—then you could pray fervently to them. If you don't already have something, then you could try using the image I've included in the insert titled "Refuge Visualization." The great, wise, loving emptiness is hard for us to relate to directly, so an image can really help. This one is of the primordial buddha (Sanskrit for "awakened one") in male and female form—our original source—our original mother and father.

I hope all this helps you. After all, the whole point is to *clear away* obscurations, and given what you know now, wouldn't you be really sad to see all or part of your efforts go to waste?

❋ *More Support—Why Not?*

While you're spending your time plumbing the depths of these understandings and practices, I encourage you to read other books and go to teaching and practice retreats. (As the band U2 notes in one of its songs: "You don't have to go it alone.")

True, practicing alone has its particular rewards, but you can get other benefits from practicing and discussing in a group. Why not have both? If there's a Vajrayana group in your area that you feel an affinity with, try one of their meetings. If not, you might put an ad in the paper (or on the Internet) and start your own study group, using this book and others I've mentioned.

If you need help finding others to practice and study with, you can contact the Namchak Foundation (www.namchak.org) and we can help you locate students near you. Over the years I've found that by sitting with others and studying and practicing together, you're much more likely to make much more progress. In fact, without the support of fellow travelers, I found that almost every single student stopped altogether.

In my own experience, of course, Tulku Sangak Rinpoche is an expert at all of these practices, he's the world lineage holder, and his motivation is impeccable. His teaching is both laser-sharp and utterly kindhearted, his sense of humor and play unfailing. I know for sure that he exemplifies the teachings in his life story and behavior. These days Rinpoche doesn't teach the foundational practices very often, but he has asked me to. If you'd like to come to one of my retreats, please do visit the Namchak website.*

In recent years, Rinpoche has asked his brother, Khen Rinpoche—a scholar and highly accomplished practitioner—to teach the foundational practices, along with others. The brothers are very much alike, not only in their practical, laser-sharp presentation, but in their kind hearts and ready laughter. You can learn more about Khen Rinpoche on the Namchak website.

I've appreciated sticking mainly with one teacher who can teach me everything, and one particular lineage, so that I don't waste too much time with distraction along the path. The downside for you is that as a result I don't have much experience of other Sanghas and teachers. Though I've heard of several Sanghas and teachers in America, I hesitate to recommend any one of them I

---

* Missoula, MT, practitioners can visit the ewam.org website.

haven't experienced myself and can't confidently give my recommendation for.

I will recommend a few resources below that I do know about, but my knowledge is limited.

That said, the books that I recommend can really help you along the way—and keep your monkey mind entertained! Of course they'll enrich your practice and your view of reality. Beyond that you'll encounter the wisdom of great masters, both past and present. Why not let them help you directly with your practice?

The other thing I want to stress, as you do these practices, is the importance of studying with actual, qualified masters. Even if you don't have one in a neighborhood near you, you can still make leaps and bounds of progress in your practice with their help by reading a book they've written, or traveling to one of their retreats.

And only qualified masters can teach you the next level of practices, the Ngöndro. Once you've decided to really give these a try, then you need to give yourself a chance to feel their effects.

Do yourself a favor, then, and—for now—resist the temptation to move on to teachings on yet other practices. If you try to move ahead too quickly, you'll risk letting these foundational practices go to waste without having really given them a chance to work—or perhaps without even fully absorbing them, like studying quadratic equations before being reliably able to multiply and divide.

The result will almost certainly be distraction from forward motion on your journey—a waste of your precious time. Probably the most important loss would be that you would have started building the walls of the house before finishing the foundation.

So, be here now, and stay here for a while.

Some of my fellow Sangha members wondered how I'd made such steady progress on the path. There were three reasons, none mysterious or impressive:

1. I stayed with one practice and just focused on that until Rinpoche gave me the next one.

2. I didn't go to any teachings or empowerments—even Rinpoche's—that weren't "on topic" for what I was actually studying or practicing at the time.

3. I spent a whole lot of time doing practice and trying my best.

   (Hint: I made the most progress on retreats. Just as total immersion is really the best way to learn a new language, total immersion in the practices works best too, for the same reasons.)

Given how precious *all* of the teachings and empowerments are, you might be wondering why I chose such a focused, seemingly narrow and restricted approach, why I decided to follow ONE path up the mountain, despite the fact that many of them would lead me there.

Well, I was daunted by the hours it would take to apply even the foundational practices to the challenge of changing the habits of my mind. When we hear about the various practices, texts, and empowerments, we can feel like a kid in a candy store (or a vegan at an organic farmers market): so many delightful options, and we want to sample them all. But I thought that my most direct route to the most potent practices and eventual enlightenment was to focus on one particular set of practices, laid out by my Root Lama, and to pursue them without any sidetracks. I believe that even Dharma can be a distraction if it's not on our own particular, step-by-step path.

Empowerments

Before I give you the names of some teachers, I want to offer another piece of advice. As you explore Vajrayana, you'll probably encounter a concept called *wang** in Tibetan, or "empowerment" in English. Again, in most cases I'd think twice before giving in to the temptation to dash off to one of these empowerments. I'll explain wangs more fully in a future book, but for now I'll just say that they can sometimes be another distraction at best. Since at a wang you're making a deep connection between your mind and the lama's, you want to be very sure this is what you want—and that lama is who you want to connect with.

Since you're also deeply connecting with a deity at a wang, you want to make sure you really plan to uphold the vows you take at that time—and, at wangs, there always are vows. The breaking of vows is not exactly good karma.

One common vow is to do the practice the wang was intended for, every day for the rest of your life. I knew one practitioner who had gone to many wangs. She would sit with a huge pile of practice texts from the various empowerments, spending so many hours keeping her accumulated vows every day that she never had a chance to finish her Ngöndro, much less the practices beyond that, even after many years.

With that caution in mind, there are some very basic empowerments that just bring the blessings of enlightened beings to you, without heavy commitments or prerequisites. The category to look in, at this point, would be the ones from the Outer Tantras. Some—though not all—of the Green Tara, Chenrezi (Avalokiteshvara), Medicine Buddha, Amitabha, and Amitayus empowerments would fall into this category. Be sure to ask about vows and prerequisites before deciding to go. Do your best to make sure the lama is one you want to have that deep, mind-to-mind connection with. If you're satisfied that there are no drawbacks to going—no excessive commitments that you can't realistically keep, no prerequisites

---

*   *Abisheka* in Sanskrit, sometimes called "transmission" in English. It is a ceremony empowering someone to pursue a particular path of practice, and to enter the mandala—the inner world, so to speak—of a particular deity.

you haven't met, no doubts about the lama leading the empower-ment—then you might as well take in the benefits.

The *reasons* to go to a wang are many and compelling. First of all, since the qualified vajra master giving the wang has joined his or her mind with the lamas of the lineage before, tracing all the way back to the Primordial Buddha, the blessings are huge. Through extremely refined and skillful means, the enlightened minds of these beings are transferred to you. It's as though a seed for enlightenment is planted within your mindstream, as are the particular archetypal qualities of the deities involved, who are also enlightened beings.

Often you will need the wang to open up your mindstream to a whole cycle of teachings, if you intend to do any study or practice within that cycle. For all of these reasons I hope that you do go to the occasional empowerment. While I was doing the Ngöndro, I went to Outer Tantra wangs for very few deities, mostly the ones included in the Ngöndro practices. Since in this case there were no vows to do some added practice, I just received the blessings of the lama, the lineages, and the deities. I need all the support I can get, in improving my mind, so I was delighted to see how much these wangs boosted my efforts.

❀ *Refuge Ceremony*

If you decide that you want to pursue this path further, then one thing that *will* help you, at this point and in the future, is the Refuge Ceremony. For that you'll need a qualified lama. I've been using the term *qualified lama* a lot but haven't defined it yet. I will go into that in the "Guru Yoga" section of Book III of this series, so when you have that, you can sneak a peek there before deciding on a Refuge Ceremony. You can also read about the attributes of a qualified lama in the first part of *The Words of My Perfect Teacher.*

Through such a lama you can connect your mind with the lineage of Buddhist masters all the way back to the Buddha. You get the support of that connection for the rest of your life and plant the seeds of enlightenment for the future. All of this happens in the Refuge Ceremony. Once you're ready, you might want to avail yourself of it. If so, it wouldn't hurt to read the corresponding chapter in *The Words of My Perfect Teacher,* and I'll have a chapter on refuge in Book II.

❀ *More About the Three Jewels*

You might be wondering exactly *what*, in the Refuge Ceremony, you'll be taking refuge *in*. Well, it won't be the things of Samsara— that's what you're taking refuge *from*. We've tried that for a few billion aeons and it hasn't really worked out. We might do well to pick something beyond the bounds of Samsara, something most likely to succeed.

If you're going on a long, confusing, sometimes difficult journey, you'll want a few essentials. First would be a guide—not just any guide, but someone who has successfully traveled to your destination. A distant second choice might be someone who hasn't gotten all the way there themselves but is confident that they know how to get there. In this case, the Buddha is obviously the first choice: he has fully succeeded in reaching the goal of liberation. For this reason he's the first of the Three Jewels.

Second, you'll want some advice and information on how to reach your destination: a map, directions about the tricky parts, and advice on how to successfully move along down the road. And, of course, you're going to need a vehicle, too. All this corresponds to the second Jewel, the Dharma. The Buddha not only traversed the path to enlightenment, he showed us the path, in several styles—Theravada, Mahayana, and Vajrayana (remember, *yana* means "vehicle"). And there are subgroups within those groups (a vehicle lot full of an array of road-tested choices, complete with Samsaric windshield wipers).

And you'll want traveling companions. Traveling alone is more arduous, not much fun, and sometimes outright dangerous. So the third Jewel is the Sangha. If you pick friends who are going in a different direction than you're headed, with a different goal, how is that going to help you on the way to *your* goal? This is a painful truth sometimes, but I couldn't not mention it to you. Please take a good, honest look at who you're marinating your mind with these days.

Thoughts and points of view are infectious.

Once you've found your traveling companions, you'll have resources you can share, you'll encourage each other when one of you gets discouraged, and you'll keep each other enthused about the journey and the goal. If one of you stumbles or gets hurt, the others will be there to help. Then there's the sheer joy of sharing the wonders of the journey. When you experience something in practice—joyful or painful—a fellow Sangha member will understand in a particular way. They might even have something especially helpful for you, because they share much of your worldview and a common "language" for talking about such things.

A variety of factors contribute to the powerful human instinct for groupthink. We like to see ourselves as above that, but biology and instinct create a very powerful tide pulling us into, and holding us within, the group. Humans have been herd animals for millions of years. For almost every bit of that time, being outside the tribe meant certain death. Jung invented many new terms as he mapped out the human psyche for us Westerners. One term, *centroversion,* is the human tendency to think like those around us.

While identifying with the group can be motivating and reassuring, once a practitioner is quite accomplished, it's recommended that they get beyond the gravitational pull of other people. At a certain point, when we're really starting to move beyond an ordinary perception of the world, sometimes even fellow Sangha members can hold us back. Then solitary retreat in a wild place is recommended.

So for you, if you're hanging out in bars a lot, do you think that would have the same effect as going to Sangha meetings and practicing together, talking about life in ways you all understand, working together on some projects, and studying Dharma books together?

I'm not suggesting you get up from reading this book and promptly divorce your husband and drop your friends. But if you'd like some support on your journey, I recommend that you find a group in your area. If there is no group, you could always start one. Remember that our website can help you find either an existing group, or other people interested in starting one. We also have audio, visual, and written materials to make it easier to start and conduct a group.

Speaking of Sangha, I thought I should mention my own. The entire Sangha is international, with monasteries and lay communities in Asia as well as the U.S. The spiritual leader of all of our communities is Tulku Sangak Rinpoche, because he is the world lineage holder of the Namchak Lineage.

Some of our centers, not surprisingly, have *Namchak* in their names, while others have the word *Ewam*. Both names have been used historically to describe our lineage, and they're all part of this larger Sangha, under Rinpoche's spiritual leadership.

You can also visit www.namchak.org for a brief history of our lineage, a "family tree" of the lineage holders tracing back to Guru Rinpoche, and more up-to-date information on the centers and the various activities. We also have an online store where you can browse for practice items, beautiful scroll paintings called *tangkas*, CDs, DVDs, and books. See you there!

What Will Refuge in the Three Jewels Do for Me?

You can get some idea from the explanations above. Beyond that, though, there is the subtle but huge support of *all* those who have ever taken refuge in those same Three Jewels. That's a lot of people. It includes all those who achieved Buddhahood, and all of the bodhisattvas. The numbers are impossible to count.

According to Sheldrake's theory of morphic resonance, that non-local wisdom, compassion, and support are there for you wherever you are. The ceremony plugs you into that greater Sangha—and that's a really big Sangha!

Once you've vowed to take refuge in those Three Jewels, you renew that vow every day. This serves to strengthen that plugging-in to the legions of wise ones and fellow travelers. It's not easy, by any means, to crowbar ourselves out of our entrenched habits. It's not even easy to do daily meditation. Heck, we have trouble even quieting our minds for a whole breath! I don't know about you, but I want all the help I can get. Remember …

Thoughts and points of view are infectious.

Might as well have that work *for* us.

And when the things of Samsara that we find ourselves secretly leaning on let us down—and sooner or later they always do—in the end, this is something we can turn to, something we can count on.

Sure, it's not easy to see, taste, or feel the Three Jewels … in the beginning. That's why they're represented in various ways—to help us find a way to perceive them. For example, the picture of the Happy Couple, as I call them, which I gave you for Shamata

practice, represents the Three Jewels. They're enlightened beings, so their minds are the Jewel of the Buddha, their speech is the Dharma, and their bodies are the Sangha.

The same is true of your Root Lama: their body is the Sangha, their speech is the Dharma, and their mind, on an ultimate level, is Buddha Mind. Because of who they are, and all the work they've done, less gets in the way of your seeing that. Of course, how well you can see the Three Jewels manifested in them still largely depends on the level of your own obscurations on and your own capacity for what's called *pure vision*.

You want to practice that with your fellow Sangha members, too. That won't always be easy. That's why they call it *practice*. But it's a very worthy cause. Just think: If you all practiced pure vision with each

other, how lovely that would feel for all of you. And your work would go well too. This is absolutely a part of the path. As a matter of fact, purifying our vision is a major feature of Vajrayana.

🌀 *How Will I Know If I'm Ready to Take Refuge?*

I have no idea.

Sorry. I can only tell you when I felt *I* was ready. When I had looked at other paths and found they weren't for me, and this one made sense to me, I decided to road-test it. And I felt the only way to do that was to actually plunge in and experience it fully. At that point I took refuge and dived into the practices, met with others, took occasional teachings, and studied. All of these elements supported and guided me, and I found that this path was really helping me. I don't know how else I would have known for sure.

🌀 *More Follow-Through: Some Qualified Teachers*

Back to the teaching retreats: they *will* help you. Obviously you want ones that focus on the practices you've been reading about, as well as those that give you more general background on Buddhism. If you like the approach of Vajrayana (Tibetan Buddhism), you'll want to focus on ones that fall within that. The Dharma is so vast that you could easily get confused if you sample different approaches without exploring any one of them fully or deeply. Since the Buddha intended for each yana to fit a particular type of person, the concepts of one can sometimes seem to contradict the other. You do want to make sure you've found the yana that works for you, but once you've done so, stick with it. Interestingly, His Holiness the Dalai Lama advises this approach even more broadly to followers of non-Buddhist spiritual traditions: if it (whatever religion or philosophy *it* may be) is working for you, you're probably best off continuing to follow its precepts.

Our Namchak Foundation, as well as Ewam, offers teaching retreats on the basic practices offered in this book, as well as others. Tulku Sangak Rinpoche himself taught them for many years, but now he focuses more on the advanced practices. We need him to! His brother, Khen Rinpoche, teaches more advanced practices and some that beginners can do as well.

Rinpoche has asked me to teach the foundational ones included in this book as well as such topics as the Seven Point Mind Training, which is also a foundational practice that takes the practices I've introduced in this book and helps us apply them to our everyday lives. I've mentioned that I teach the Ngöndro, or Preliminary Practices, as well. I would recommend doing the practices in this book for at least six months to a year before moving on to the Ngöndro. Of course you're welcome to come to any of our beginning-level retreats that are appropriate. (If you're not sure whether a retreat would be a good fit for you, please contact us—or whoever might be holding the retreat, if it's elsewhere—and ask.)

I'd be happy to see you there! We do a lot of learning, learn a lot of doing, and have a lot of fun doing it.

If you can't or don't want to go to one of those offered through the Namchak Foundation or Ewam, you could go to one offered by Anam Thubten Rinpoche. He is also both an erudite scholar and an accomplished practitioner. An added benefit is that he speaks excellent English.

Another qualified master is Mingyur Rinpoche, and he teaches this level, as do some of his advanced students. He also speaks English, and of course his American students who teach do, too!

Dzigar Kongtrül Rinpoche gives excellent Dharma talks every Sunday on the Web. These could help you with your background information. His book *It's Up to You* is direct and pithy and really helps you to take a good look at your mind. I assume his Sangha offers teaching retreats, but I don't know what levels. I'm less familiar with him or his Sangha.

Speaking of Dharma talks on the Web, we are planning to set Tulku Sangak Rinpoche up to do that as well—through a translator, of course. Visit our website to see when that's available.

There are probably other qualified teachers of beginning Vajrayana out there, but as I said, I don't get out much. I don't feel I can recommend a teacher or Sangha without having some personal experience of them and their teachings—so if I don't mention here someone who appeals to you, I'm not *not* recommending them; I just don't know enough to have an informed opinion (which is really the best kind to have).

Sogyal Rinpoche's book, *The Tibetan Book of Living and Dying*, is a great introduction that gives a lot of stories and other information, including the Tibetan understanding of the dying process and the bardo that follows. He has many centers all over the world and is quite famous. I've never visited one of his Sanghas so I can't comment on them, but I highly recommend his book.

The Next Step—When You're Really Ready

I'm hoping this book helps you be a happier person. That would make *me* happy.

If you read this book, try the methods for a while, and find you're really interested in pursuing this path further, you'll need some support on your way.

First and most essentially, as I've said, you'll need a qualified teacher. Second, you'll want to take the Refuge Vows.

Third, once you've done these practices for at least six months to a year, and if you want to pursue Vajrayana, the traditional next step is the Ngöndro, or "Preliminary Practices." The word doesn't refer to their being simple or remedial. They're a collection of practices that are a microcosm of the entire Vajrayana path. They're considered so essential that they're done either at the beginning of, or before, any other practices, and before starting one's day. *That's* what's meant by *preliminary*.

The Ngöndro practice texts are specifically designed to be supports and reminders for the *lama's teachings*. In many cases even though the teacher may not have been ordained a lama, they will still be highly qualified. You simply have to look at their qualifications, both inner and outer, and judge if they're right for you. The Ngöndro text in my next book is meant almost as a reminder or reference—to bring the lama's full teachings to mind when you're doing your daily practice. It's not meant to replace the lama's live teachings—and neither is this book, for that matter (although I am a live lama!).

Without that personal, in-person interaction with a teacher, you're missing crucial pieces and the Ngöndro simply won't work for you in the way it's intended. The Ngöndro is strong medicine, and you don't want to take it without seeing the doctor and getting their instructions.

The practices I give in this book can be done without a qualified teacher's instruction without much risk of harm. But if you try them and like them, why not get more support, help, and clarity from a qualified teacher for these, too? This book, together with the other two books in the series, is not the only reading you'll need, either. In Appendix C: Recommended Reading, I list and talk a bit about some excellent books that can further your understanding.

And for those of you who find this is your cup of tea and would like to learn and practice further, the second and third books in this series will present the next set of practices. The medicine gets progressively stronger as we go along. Rinpoche has taught me all of the levels of this path, as he has for many others. Not only has he authorized me to teach all of the foundational practices, he fully *expects* me to teach them. That works for me—there's nothing I like better!

For now you have quite a few new understandings, methods, and resources—congratulations! It's a little like you've been given recipes, and you even have the ingredients. Now if you cook them up and actually *eat* them ... then give yourself some time to *chew and digest* ... wouldn't that be lovely? Isn't that the best part of a recipe?

In the large view you've now considered, you might ask yourself the question I've asked myself so many times, over the years:

"Do I have something *better* to do?"

Appendix A: How to Find or Start a Group

Here are a few ideas to help you find fellow adventurers, and to help you all begin and continue the exploration together.

Of course you can all use this book as part of that exploration. You can read a bit during the week, then gather in someone's living room to discuss that bit, seeing what gem of understanding you create when you share all your varied facets of understanding.

To keep things focused, I recommend following the simple procession of events I've outlined below. You could trade off being the person to lead you all through it. When I was doing three-month-long retreats, that's what our weekly group did. At the beginning of the three months, each member signed up for a particular time. It worked quite well, and everyone became very close.

During the meetings you can talk together about each of your life's challenges and how these understandings and methods are, or aren't, working for you. You offer each other your simple, caring support.

Then you meditate together, a beautiful experience like none other—sharing the silence. I've included a simple guide below that leaves lots of room for your own group's creativity and personality.

But how do you find such a group if you don't happen to have one handy? This modern world, where we don't even know most of our neighbors' names, doesn't make it easy. But there's a very modern solution: the Internet. On our website (www.namchak.org) you can find others in your ZIP code or nearby ones, and see if a few people there would like to get together. Chances are they do—why else would they have registered on the website? Of course there are lots of other Internet and social media possibilities for finding people to share this adventure.

On the website you'll also find more advice on how to conduct and manage meetings, blogs you can join or just read, information about our presence on Twitter, Facebook, etc., as well as a little custom we've developed of "offering a flower." Are you intrigued? Check it out!

As I've said in various ways in this book, I believe that our modern society got confused along the way. We made the mistake of substituting money for meaning. This served to isolate us. We became isolated from the human beings around us, the other beings around us, and the whole environment. Has this served to bring us happiness? We thought it would, but we have come to the logical end of this pursuit. It hasn't brought us our desired goal of happiness, but is destroying the planet, creatures, other people, and left us with little meaning to our lives. Many have found that these simple little living room study groups have brought deep meaning and connection to their lives. I wish that for you.

Meanwhile, here's a very simple template to use with a group—a learning community, as I think of it—with this or another book as a basis of study.

❋ Practice Group Meeting

- ❋ A few minutes of silence.

- ❋ Give rise to Bodhicitta motivation—the Two Purposes: enlightenment for self and others.

- ❋ Each person checks in:

  How is everyone doing with practice/life?
  How is everyone doing with the practice of Doing Daily Practice?
  And how have you connected that with last week's reading?

- ❋ Read a few pages from a selected text.

- ❋ Discuss.

- ❋ Round Robin Meditation for 20 minutes.

- ❋ Dedication and Aspiration.

- ❋ A few minutes of chanting, if you like.

❋ Dedication/Aspiration

By the power of this compassionate practice
May suffering be transformed into peace.
May the hearts of all beings be open,
And their wisdom radiate from within.

Appendix B: Glossary

Working Definitions of Buddhist (and Other) Terms

Absolute Truth: The abiding truth, not subject to a particular deluded being's point of view. The reality perceived by enlightened beings. *See also* Two Truths.

Archetype: Jungian term describing a sort of lens that acts as a template, shaping generalized consciousness into a more particular principle of reality with particular characteristics—for example, the Great Mother archetype or the Wise Man archetype—which one can find in images and stories throughout human societies.

Bardo (Tibetan; literally, "between two"): Generally used to refer to the dreamlike state between lifetimes. Technically we experience other bardos, such as the time in between birth and death.

Bodhicitta *[bo-di-CHIT-ta]* (Sanskrit; "Mind of Enlightenment/Awakening"): (from *The Words of My Perfect Teacher,* by Patrul Rinpoche, trans., Padmakhara Translation Group): "On the relative level, it is the wish to attain Buddhahood for the sake of all beings, as well as the practice of the path of love, compassion, the six transcendent perfections, etc., necessary for achieving that goal. On the absolute level, it is the direct insight into the ultimate nature." It is the motivation to help others. It naturally flows from our own Buddha Nature, which *feels* how we're not separate from others.

Bodhisattva *[bo-di-SAT-va]* (Sanskrit): One who is primarily motivated by Bodhicitta. There are many levels of bodhisattva, depending on the spiritual achievement of such a being.

Buddha (Sanskrit; "Awakened One"): A being who has reached full enlightenment by cleansing all adventitious *lo-bur* ("baggage") such as karma and bad habits of the mind, and has fully brought forth—matured—their Buddha Nature. It is predicted that there will be over a thousand who will reach this state in this kalpa, or aeon. Note: The buddha who created the religion and methods of Buddhism and taught the sutras and tantras was the Buddha Shakyamuni.

Buddha Nature (Tibetan; *deshek nyingpo*): Our essential nature, which is not separate from the Dharmakaya and is the seed of our own complete enlightenment.

Dharma (Sanskrit): A general term for the teachings and path of the Buddha Shakyamuni.

Dharmakaya (Sanskrit; literally, "Truth Body"): The vast, pregnant emptiness out of which everything arises. It is not a dead vacuum, but pure, essential awareness. It is beyond defining but has many qualities. It is vast without limit, ultimate compassion, ultimate unity, pure potential, all-knowing, the ultimate root of all. At this level there is no form; there is unity. It is no different from complete Buddhahood.

Five Dhyani Buddha Families: For each of these five categories, or families, there is a particular buddha, color, direction, and many other characteristics:

1. Buddha.
2. Vajra.
3. Jewel.
4. Lotus.
5. Karma (Enlightened Activity).

These are also listed in the same order as the Five Poisons. The Five Buddha

Families weave together, along with all their qualities and characteristics, to create the complex appearances of manifested reality.

Five Poisons: The five neurotic emotions which usually motivate the thoughts, speech, and actions of sentient beings. The Buddha spoke of 84,000 of them, but they are generally grouped into these categories:

1. Clinging, desire, longing, addiction, etc.
2. Aversion, aggression, fear, hatred, worry, etc.
3. Ignorance, stupor, laziness, dullness, narrow-mindedness, etc.
4. (A subcategory of #3) Pride, ego inflation.
5. (Also a subcategory of #3) Jealousy, competitiveness.

When we speak of the *Three Poisons*, we're to understand that #4 and #5 are subsumed under #3.

Five Primordial Yeshes: The first division into multiplicity; emanating from the unified nature of the Dharmakaya. Yeshe divides into its five basic aspects, like facets of one jewel. This is on the Sambhogakaya level. Each of the Five Poisons, without its adventitious, deluded element—in other words, in its pure essence—is one of the Five Primordial Yeshes. Below they are listed in the order in which the Five Poisons were listed:

1. Discerning Yeshe.
2. Mirrorlike Yeshe.
3. Yeshe of Basic Space.
4. Equalizing Yeshe.
5. All-Accomplishing Yeshe.

Four Thoughts: The longer term is "Four Thoughts That Turn the Mind (From Samsara)." This is a group of four contemplations that, from four different entry points, guide us in a thorough exploration of our larger situation within Samsara.

Karma (Sanskrit; "action"): In this context it refers not only to actions but to their natural consequential effects. Think "Ye shall reap what ye sow."

Lama (Tibetan): A title equivalent to *rabbi* or *minister*. In Vajrayana the lama is often more of a spiritual mentor than their Christian counterpart or than in Theravada Buddhism.

Mahayana (Sanskrit; "Great Vehicle"): That branch of Buddhism which has the Two Purposes as motivating factors: Enlightenment for self *and* for others. In every school of Mahayana Buddhism, one takes a vow to help *all* beings toward enlightenment.

Marigpa (Tibetan): Lack of awareness. Usually translated as "ignorance."

Merit: Positive effects of actions, in particular. Like some entry appearing in the credit column of the karmic "ledger."

Mindstream: That bit of awareness that inhabits the body but isn't actually *of* the body, and that experiences lifetime after lifetime.

Ngöndro *[ngön-dro]* (Tibetan; "Preliminary Practices"): These are practiced after Shiney and before more advanced practices. Actually, Ngöndro is incorporated into the beginning of advanced practices too—hence the name.

Nirmanakaya (Sanskrit; "Emanation Body"): The manifestation level/aspect of shining forth from the Dharmakaya/Buddhahood. Another, further order of complexity of form, as compared with the Sambhogakaya. Perceptible to sentient beings in a warped and confused way, depending on their own karmically and habitually distorted "lens."

Original Purity (Tibetan; *kadak*): An intrinsic quality of the Dharmakaya, and all that issues from it. This, of course, includes human beings.

Relative Truth: The reality perceived by sentient beings, in their deluded state. *See also* Two Truths.

Rinpoche *[RIN-po-chey]*: An honorific term used for high lamas—higher than the Christian term *Reverend*, but lower than *His Holiness*. Most lamas are not referred to by this title, only the most accomplished.

Root Lama: Root guru. Our individual spiritual guide and mentor. This is arguably the most intimate and karmically significant of human relationships.

Sambhogakaya (Sanskrit; literally, "Body of Complete Enjoyment"): The first level/aspect of spontaneous shining forth into form, from the Dharmakaya. Similar to the archetypal level of being that Jungians speak of. Rarely directly perceptible to human beings.

Samsara (Sanskrit): The cycle of existence, of birth, death, and rebirth, in which all sentient beings find ourselves. We are propelled from one situation to the next by our own deluded thoughts, negative emotions, karma, and habits of mind, from which we perform actions which, in turn, create further karmic consequences. We then react to these, mentally, emotionally, and physically. These in turn create ceaseless experiences in existence, like a self-perpetuating dream, until we finally wake up (and, as His Holiness the Dalai Lama says, "Better it be sooner").

Sangha (Sanskrit): The spiritual community.

Shamata (Sanskrit; "Tranquil Abiding Meditation"): A meditation which is practiced, in similar forms, in all branches of Buddhism. It is taught to new practitioners in Vajrayana. Its endeavor is to calm the flow of thoughts while heightening mindfulness. Eventually, through this training, one can focus attention on one thing and have it stay there, in a clear, unperturbed, joyfully peaceful state.

Sublime Insight (Sanskrit; *Pali, Vipassana, Vipashyana*): This is usually practiced in conjunction with Tranquil Abiding, Shamata. Both of these practices are found in all branches of Buddhism. In Vajrayana they're seen as foundational and necessary, but as a means to further practices. In a commonly used metaphor, Shamata and Vipassana are like the foundation of a house, which must be well established before the walls and the roof are added.

Sutra *[SOO-tra]*: The original teachings of the Buddha.

Tantra *[TAHN-tra]*: Further teachings of the Buddha, which are not studied or practiced by the Theravadins but are the mainstay of Vajrayana—Tibetan Buddhism.

Theravada *[teh-ra-VA-da]* (Sanskrit; "Root, or Foundational Vehicle, School of the Elders"): The foundational level branch of Buddhism, common to all branches. Of the three main branches of teachings of the Buddha Shakyamuni, it was the first to be taught. It is based on the sutras, and does not include the tantras; the motivation for enlightenment is focused on one's own liberation from Samsara.

Three Jewels: The Buddha, the Dharma, and the Sangha—in which all Buddhists have vowed to take refuge until reaching complete enlightenment. The thought is that the combination of all three will greatly help us along the way: the Buddha because he has achieved enlightenment himself, so has proven to know the way; the Dharma because it is the instructions, or "map," that he provided us; and the Sangha, or spiritual community, as companions along the way.

Three Kayas: *See* Dharmakaya, Samboghakaya, Nirmanakaya.

Three Poisons, a.k.a. *Afflictive Emotions* (Tibetan; *Nyönmong*): The Buddha (Shakyamuni) grouped the thousands of emotions like fear, worry, longing, etc., into three basic categories:

1. Ignorance, delusion, laziness, narrow-mindedness, and similar emotions.
2. Desire, clinging, longing, and such.
3. Aversion, aggression, hatred, dislike, fear, and such.

Sometimes these are spoken of as the Five Poisons, with the fourth and fifth categories under the third category, aversion/aggression. The fourth is pride, inflation, and such, and the fifth is jealousy, competitiveness, and such. They are often subsumed under the third category because they are considered to be forms, subsets, of aversion/aggression.

Three Yanas: See *Theravada, Mahayana, Vajrayana.*

Tonglen (Tibetan; "Sending and Receiving"): A compassion practice in which one breathes in the suffering of others and breathes out toward them one's wishes for their happiness.

Tulku *[TOOL-koo]* (Tibetan; "Emanation Body." Sanskrit; *Nirmanakaya*); An individual who has mastered their mind enough that they can control their landing in their next incarnation. The tulku system has been used in Tibet for heads of monasteries and sub-lineages, to allow them to shoulder their responsibilities for many lifetimes. This is why His Holiness the Dalai Lama XIV is referred to as the 14th: he has been recognized and has held the Office of the Dalai Lama thirteen previous times.

Two Truths (Tibetan; *denba nyi*): The two aspects of reality, like two sides of one coin. These two aspects are called Relative Truth (*kün dzop denba*) and Absolute Truth, or Ultimate Truth (*dön dam denba*).

Vajrayana: A branch of Mahayana, which uses many skillful means from the tantras to pursue enlightenment more efficiently.

Vipassana (Tibetan; *Lhaktong*. English; "Sublime Insight"): Usually practiced along with Shamata/Shiney. The practice of seeing the true nature of either the object of our attention or us ourselves.

Wang, Lung: These are two kinds of transmissions that a lama gives to students, to connect and open their minds in a profound way to a particular cycle of teachings and/or practices.

Yeshe: Also called Timeless Awareness or (Primordial) Wisdom. The wisdom inherent in the Dharmakaya, which shines forth into all of its created emanations.

Yidam: Deity practice. One meditates on a particular realized being who personifies a particular aspect of wisdom—an archetypal image. It is widely practiced in Vajrayana.

Appendix C: Recommended Reading

For Practice and General Reading

Tulku Sangak Rinpoche. *The Way to Practice Tranquil Abiding.* Missoula, MT: Namchak Publishing, in press. Most books on Shiney/Shamata are coming from the slightly different presentation of the Theravada or Mahayana traditions. This is by my lama, a Vajrayana master, so it's a great preparation for anyone who is thinking of continuing on with the Vajrayana path. You can purchase this through our website: namchak.org.

Matthieu Ricard. *Happiness.* New York: Little Brown & Co. English language edition, 2006. This book does a beautiful job of answering the question, "Tibetan Buddhism—why bother?" Ricard was at Dilgo Khyentse Rinpoche's side since before Tulku Sangak Rinpoche arrived, and he is still at Khyentse Rinpoche's monastery. He is one of the monks the scientists have conducted experiments on, so he's certified as a good meditator! The book is simply a joy to read and a perfect one to hand out to friends and family with whom you'd like to begin sharing all this.

In 2010 he followed *Happiness* with a book called *Why Meditate?* which includes a CD. I think this could be a very helpful aid for anyone who would actually like to give meditation a go. Again, he's a Vajrayana master, so his would be an excellent preparation for those who like this path.

David R. Loy. *The World Is Made of Stories*. Boston: Wisdom Publications, 2010. In this pithy book, Loy poetically shows us JUST how much our experience is a movie of our own making.

Dacher Keltner, Jason Marsh, and Jeremy Adam Smith. *The Compassionate Instinct*. New York: W. W. Norton, 2010. Through stories and studies, the authors reveal the Buddha Nature in us all, ready to come forth at any time, often at surprising times.

Stephen Post, Ph.D., and Jill Neimark. *Why Good Things Happen to Good People*. New York: Broadway Books, 2008. This scientifically grounded book is an accessible, enjoyable read. Inspiring. The main study they refer to is a longitudinal study that involves in-depth annual interviews of the subjects over their entire adult lives.

Shantideva. Trans. Padmakara Translation Group. *The Way of the Bodhisattva*. Boston: Shambhala Publications, 2006. This is the all-time classic for advice on how to bring Bodhicitta into your life. Lots of helpful, grounded metaphors and reframes.

Sharon Salzberg and Joseph Goldstein. *Insight Meditation: A Step-by-Step Course on How to Meditate*. Boulder, CO: Sounds True, 2001. This is a complete multimedia kit that is the best, most accessible introduction that I know of, for Westerners just starting to meditate. I find it helpful too! It's not Vajrayana style, though, so you might want to keep your eyes and mouth open, etc., as I've instructed you in this book. Joseph Goldstein has written other books with the same title, but I thought you might want this kit, put out by Sounds True. Interestingly, both authors are also Dzogchen (Vajrayana) meditators. They have been involved in the Mind and Life group (scientists and the Dalai Lama) for many years.

Sangharakshita. *What Is the Sangha?: The Nature of the Spiritual Community*. Cambridge, UK: Windhorse Publications, 2004. Sangharakshita is a Westerner, deeply steeped in Buddhism, who can explain those understandings to the Western mind in a way that we can relate to. He's very much done it for us here with the concept of Jewel of the Sangha—not just as an understanding but as a practice.

Sangharakshita has also written *Who Is the Buddha?* (2008) and *What Is the Dharma?* (2004), so he's covered all Three Jewels!

Patrul Rinpoche. Trans. by the Padmakara Translation Group. *The Words of My Perfect Teacher.* Boston: Shambhala,1998. This is the all-time classic text for Ngöndro. It's VERY Tibetan, but if you approach it like an anthropologist, with an open, scientific mind, you're bound to find many helpful elements, including lots of stories. If you're going to practice Ngöndro, it's your text-book. If you're going to practice the Four Thoughts, it will give you plenty of, well, food for Thought.

Just about anything by Pema Chödrön, especially *Start Where You Are.* Boston: Shambhala, 2001. And, that same book turned into a beautiful little kit called *The Compassion Box.* This is an ancient course on how to bring Bodhicitta into your life, and use your life for growing your Bodhicitta. It's been popular all these years because it works. Pema Chödrön really tells it like it is, as a modern American, and at the same time is a highly qualified teacher of Vajrayana.

Anam Thubten. *No Self, No Problem.* Point Richmond, CA: Dharmata Press, 2006. This is a great little book written by a true lama, but very accessible to a Westerner. It's pithy, and full of great little gems that guide our minds in the direction we'd like them to go. He teaches Shamata regularly. He and Tulku Sangak Rinpoche are close, and teach at each other's sanghas.

Any book by Mingyur Rinpoche. He also teaches Shamata regularly, as do an increasing number of his advanced, highly qualified students. They teach Ngöndro and other practices too. You can check all of this out on his web-site, www.tergar.org.

Michael Talbot. *The Holographic Universe.* New York: Harper Perennial Reprint Edition, 2011. I've said enough about this one for you to know it's packed with one thing after another that can really alter your viewing lens, so once again I recommend you take it in sips.

Daniel Siegel. *The Mindful Brain: Reflection and Attunement in the Cultivation of Well-Being.* New York: W. W. Norton & Company, 2007. This one you'd also want to take in sips. By the end you'll have a whole different understanding of your mind and your brain—more full and more detailed, but most impor-tant, more true.

Rick Hanson, Ph.D., with Richard Mendius, M.D. *Buddha's Brain: The Practical Neuroscience of Happiness, Love, and Wisdom.* Oakland, CA: New Harbinger Publications, 2009. This is my favorite book on brain science in relationship to Buddhist meditation techniques. It really gets into the parts of the brain, what they do, how they work together, how that relates to how we feel, and how Buddhist methods can help us to use the brain in a way that allows us to practice equanimity while still feeling fully alive.

Dzigar Kongtrül. *It's Up To You: The Practice of Self-Reflection on the Buddhist Path.* Boston and London: Shambhala, 2006. This is another pithy book, full of helpful thoughts and perspectives, from a genuine lama who also speaks English.

Sogyal Rinpoche. *The Tibetan Book of Living and Dying.* New York: HarperOne, 2002. Has come to be a classic introduction for Westerners. It gives you a feel for the Tibetan perspective.

Anything (and there's a lot of it) by B. Alan Wallace. He is highly qualified to speak about Buddhism, science, and Contemplative Science. He was a monk in the Vajrayana lineage, studied under many lamas, and has translated for many of them. He then went on to get a degree in physics. Now he is one of the scholars working with His Holiness the Dalai Lama in developing the new field they call Contemplative Science. He is one of the key people doing the Shamata Project, measuring the brains and bodies of novice meditators as they do three-month intensive Buddhist retreats.

Three Books by Thubten Chodron

Buddhism for Beginners. Ithaca, NY: Snow Lion Publications, 2001.
Don't Believe Everything You Think: Living with Wisdom and Compassion. Ithaca, NY: Snow Lion Publications, 2013.
Working With Anger. Ithaca, NY: Snow Lion Publications, 2001.

Thubten Chodron is a Western Buddhist nun who speaks in a very down-to-earth way about the principles of Buddhism. Because she has applied these principles in her own life, she does a beautiful job of helping us apply them in our own.

Brain Science

Richard J. Davidson, Ph.D., with Sharon Begley. *The Emotional Life of Your Brain: How Its Unique Patterns Affect the Way You Think, Feel, and Live—and How You Can*

Change Them. New York: Plume, reprint edition, 2013. A long subtitle, but truly descriptive. Dr. Davidson is among the top neuroscientists in the growing field of Contemplative Science, which studies the effects of meditation on the brain, with full scientific rigor. He works closely with His Holiness the Dalai Lama. Given Dr. Davidson's accomplishments, we might expect to not be able to understand a thing—so it's a pleasant surprise to discover how readable and accessible this book is. Not one to leave it as an academic study, he has practiced meditation for many years. He is a living poster child of how richly we can cultivate positive habits of mind.

Seven Point Mind Training Books and Media

Before you go on to Ngöndro, I highly recommend you check out *Lojong*, a.k.a. the Seven Point Mind Training teachings. Pema Chödrön often teaches it, so you could also attend a live teaching. There are probably others who teach it, but I haven't experienced their teachings so I can't speak with authority on them. Since there are many commentaries on this classic by Chekawa Yeshe Dorje, a website—lojongmindtraining.com—offers commentaries from several masters on many of the maxims contained in the root text.

Traleg Kyabgon. *The Practice of Lojong: Cultivating Compassion Through Training the Mind*. Boston and London: Shambhala, 2007. This book is long but readable, and includes some of the relevant neuroscience.

There is video of His Holiness the Dalai Lama giving a teaching on Seven Point Mind Training.

Dilgo Khyentse Rinpoche. Trans. Padmakara. *Enlightened Courage*. Ithaca, NY: Snow Lion Publications, 1993 and 2006. Dilgo Khyentse Rinpoche was one of the great scholars and practitioners of the twentieth century. He was the head of the Nyingma Lineage, historically the most populous in Vajrayana. He lived this text to the utmost. He was able to speak its true meaning in down-to-earth terms.

Pema Chödrön. *Start Where You Are*. Boston: Shambhala, 2001. This is the most accessible for Westerners. My one quibble is that she refers to the maxims as "slogans," a term she got from Trungpa Rinpoche. If you looked up the definitions of both words, it would be "maxim," not "slogan," that would mean "words to live by." A slogan is a phrase you use to sell a car or a political candidate. Oh well, that's a minor point. I still highly recommend this book!

Pema Chödrön also has MP3s of courses and talks she has given on this training.

Pema Chödrön. *The Compassion Box*. Boston and London: Shambhala, 2003. When in doubt, get this one. It includes the above, as well as beautiful cards, with a maxim on the front and her explanation on the back. There is a little stand, so you can have it on your desk or in your kitchen, reminding you of your theme for the day.

Jamgon Kongtrül. *The Great Path of Awakening: The Classic Guide to Lojong, a Tibetan Buddhist Practice for Cultivating the Heart of Compassion*. Trans. Ken McCleod. Boston and London: Shambhala, 2005. Jamgon Kongtrül "the Great" was among the most influential masters in the nineteenth century, in Tibet. This is his commentary, beautifully translated by Ken McCleod. I turn to this one at least as much as any of the others.

Chögyam Trungpa. *Training the Mind and Cultivating Loving-Kindness*. Boston and London: Shambhala, 1993. My one quibble with this, again, is the use of "slogan" instead of "maxim." Though his English was excellent, it wasn't his first language. In the case of this one word choice, perhaps it shows. Since she was Pema Chödrön's Root Lama, it's no wonder she uses the word "slogan," despite her being American.

❁ *On Cosmology*

His Holiness the Dalai Lama. *The Universe in a Single Atom: The Convergence of Science and Sprituality*. New York: Morgan Road Books, Random House, 2005. This emerged from one of the Mind and Life meetings between prominent scientists and His Holiness the Dalai Lama. The subject of this one was cosmology. Appropriately enough for a conference on cosmology, this is a vast subject, with many scientific points of view, not all of which could be represented at that meeting. (There's information on the Mind and Life group's website in the "Websites" section below.)

❁ *On Impermanence*

Ram Dass. *Still Here*. New York: Riverhead Books, 2001. Ram Dass has been a primary spiritual leader in Western society for many decades. He writes with courageous honesty, wit, and wisdom on the subject of impermanence. Just as he was about to start the book, he almost died from a stroke. He includes that event and his arduous recovery in this book.

Sherwin B. Nuland, M.D. *How We Die: Reflections on Life's Final Chapter,* new edition. New York: Vintage, 1995. Dr. Nuland gives several examples of what is actually going on in the body when we die suddenly, or from a long illness. He writes with precision, eloquence, and compassion. He shares with us a painful universal reality with the skill of a doctor and the soul of a kind human being.

✽ *Fun and Inspiring Reading*

Anna M. Cox. *Just As the Breeze Blows Through Moonlight: The Spiritual Life Journey of Thupten Heruka, a 19th c. Tibetan Yogi.* Bloomington, IN: Xlibris, 2002. This story—both an outer and inner adventure, set in old Tibet—came to Cox after she had been a practitioner for a long time. I didn't want to put it down. I was sad when it was over and I had to leave that world. One of those rare indulgences that's good for you.

Vicki Mackenzie. *Cave In the Snow: Tenzin Palmo's Quest for Enlightenment.* New York: Bloomsbury Publishing, 1998. This is the life story of an Englishwoman who found her way to great Tibetan masters in India, then spent twelve years practicing in a cave in Lhadak. She's come back to tell us about it. Very readable and inspiring.

Ani Tenzin Palmo. *Reflections on a Mountain Lake: Teachings on Practical Buddhism.* Ithaca, NY: Snow Lion Publications, 2002. This is Ani (nun) Tenzin Palmo's own book. It's full of advice and inspiration that's lovely to take in—in sips—and savor.

✽ *Websites*

Well, of course, there's ours: www.namchak.org. We have a lot of free teachings there, opportunities to connect with others in your area and beyond, and a little Sangha store, and more. You'll recognize some of the contents of this book, and audio or video support for some of its content, including Shamata, Tonglen, and Clearing the Stale Winds. Other articles and teachings come and go, too. We also have a large and growing library of print, audio, and visual teachings from our own lamas.

A fun and intriguing one is www.spaceandmotion.com. It combines a lot of different areas of knowledge, including histories of science and various branches of philosophy. My one caveat is that the website includes what I consider some questionable "science." The scientists represented there are respected by many, though considered controversial by some. But then, so was Galileo, in his time. If you liked *The Holographic Universe*, you'll be interested in this website.

Anam Thubten's website: www.dharmata.org.

Mingyur Rinpoche's website: www.tergar.org.

For more on Seven Point Mind Training, or Lojong: www.lojongmindtraining.com.

The Mind and Life group's website offers a lot of historical and current thought on cosmology, with the goal of seeing how current scientific thought on the subject fits with Buddhist cosmology. www.mindandlife.org.

Dr. Richard J. Davidson's website: www.investigatinghealthyminds.org. This is my favorite brain science website. They are doing cutting-edge research on such fascinating topics as the measurable effects of meditation on DNA, classroom behavior improvement through meditation, and measurably positive effects on military veterans who practice meditation.

Appendix D: Credits and Permissions

This page is a continuation of the copyright page. Grateful acknowledgment is made for permission granted to reproduce images and to use quotes in the text.

PHOTOS AND IMAGES

QUOTES

PRODUCTION

Index

Lama Sangak Yeshe Tsomo

CURRICULUM VITAE

Education and Professional Training

2006–present: One to two months' retreat annually, with instruction and guidance from Tulku Sangak Rinpoche and Khen Rinpoche.

1995–present: Scores of teachings, empowerments, and pilgrimages, including the following:

- ❋ Semiannual ten-day Dzogchen instruction retreats with Tulku Sangak Rinpoche (2006–2010).

- ❋ Six years of ten-day instruction retreats on *The Treasury of Precious Qualities*, a classic text which includes the entire Buddhist path. Tulku Sangak Rinpoche, Khen Rinpoche, and Anam Thubten Rinpoche, instructors.

- ❋ Finished Ngöndro (Preliminary Practices). This involved 108,000 prostrations, 108,000 repetitions of the 100-Syllable Mantra, 1,200,000 recitations of the Vajra Guru mantra, and other similarly extensive practices.

✸ Small-group meeting with His Holiness the Dalai Lama. Ann Arbor, MI (April 2008).

✸ Tenshug offering to His Holiness the Dalai Lama. Dharamsala, India (as part of a ten-day pilgrimage, July 2007).

✸ Two interviews with His Holiness the Dalai Lama.

2005: In Nepal and 2006 in the U.S. Lama Ordination (bestowed by Tulku Sangak Rinpoche).

1995–2005: Ongoing intensive lama training in the Nyingma tradition, with Rinpoche.
The following were among the components of the training:

✸ Twenty-six one- to two-week training intensives.

✸ Traditional three-year retreat, in strict, solitary retreat conditions, under Rinpoche's direct supervision, progressing from one stage of training to the next, finishing with the highest levels of Dzogchen practice. The practice retreats were usually done three months at a time.

✸ Several months of study and training at Rinpoche's monastery in Nepal.

✸ Ongoing scholarly and spiritual study of numerous classic Vajrayana Buddhist texts.

✸ Was given increased responsibility as a teacher under Rinpoche's guidance.

✸ Learned to speak fluent Tibetan, allowing ability to chant in Tibetan while understanding the meaning, to act as translator for students and practitioners, and most important, to speak extensively with Rinpoche and Khen Rinpoche, as well as other lamas, about the Dharma.

1990: M.A., Counseling Psychology, Antioch University (emphasis: Jungian Studies).

1987: B.A., Counseling Psychology, Antioch University.

Affiliations and Memberships

Namchak Foundation, Montana. Co-founder, current board member.

Academy for the Love of Learning, Santa Fe, NM. Founding Board member.

Ewam (U.S. and international nonprofit center and school). Founding board member, board member, 1999–2004.

Light of Berotsana translation group, Boulder, CO. board member, 2002–2008.

Namchak Foundation (U.S. and international group with physical and online presence, dedicated to supporting people of the Namchak Lineage in Tibet and developing retreat sites). Co-founder with Namchak Dorlop Dorje Lopön Choeji Lodoe.

Pleasant Ridge Waldorf School, Viroqua, WI. Founder and board member, ca. 1975.

Selected Publications

The Lotus and the Rose: Conversations Between Tibetan Buddhism and Mystical Christianity, with The Rev. Dr. Matthew Fox (DVD and text), 2015.

"Ani Tsering Wangmo: A Life of Merit" in *Lion's Roar Newsletter*, March 2010.

"Coming Home" in *Originally Blessed*. Oakland, CA: Creation Spirituality Communities, 2008.

"Dharmasala" in *Lion's Roar Newsletter*, August 2007.

"Shedra" in *Lion's Roar Newsletter*, February 2006.

Selected Presentations and Teachings

Three-hour introduction to Tibetan Buddhism, shown on TV in Taiwan. This was posted on YouTube in five installments.

A variety of teachings, including weekly and short retreats (2005–present) when on site at the Ewam center and at other U.S. and international sites.

Two guest appearances at the University of Montana School of Social Work, 2011.

"Once Existing from Self, Your Life Target Will Come Out Like Art Creation" (presentation to educators, students, artists, and general public). Miaolie Pottery. Miaolie, Taiwan. May 2010.

"Solving Confusion in the Mind" (presentation to Taiwan Sunshine Women's Association). Taichung Ewam Centre. Taichung, Taiwan. May 2010.

"Experience Sharing: To Change Your Life and Career from Miserable to Successful by Learning the Methods of Mind Observation Training" (talk to 25 business owners and senior managers). Howard Hotel. Taipei, Taiwan. April 2010.

"Learning Buddhism" retreat. Taichung Ewam Centre. Taichung, Taiwan. April 2010.

"Learning Buddhism and Doing Practices to Clarify Confusion." Howard Hotel. Taipei, Taiwan. April 2010.

"Seven Point Mind Training." Yung Ho Training Centre. Taiwan. March 2010.

"Seven Point Mind Training, 3rd Installment," Retreat. Ewam, Arlee, MT. November 2009.

"Inner Peace/Outer Peace: What Is the Relationship?" (with Frances Moore Lappé). Peace Festival. Ewam, Arlee, MT. September 2009.

"Seven Point Mind Training, 1st Installment," retreat. Ewam, Arlee, MT. April 2009.

"Seven Point Mind Training, 2nd Installment," retreat. Ewam, Arlee, MT. May 2009.

"Organic Food and Buddhism" (presentation to second-level Buddhists). Howard Hotel. Taipei, Taiwan. March 2009.

"Enjoy Your Life with Happiness" and "From Common Happiness to Common Bodhi." Taipei Shilin Resort. Taipei, Taiwan. March 2009.

"Gratitude; Visualization; Dreams Come True, as Your Wishes." National Taiwan Normal University. Taipei, Taiwan. March 2009.

"Buddhism." Unitarian Universalist Church. Missoula, MT. May 2008.